MW01670653

NORWEGIAN-AMERICAN STUDIES

The Journal of the Norwegian American Historical Association

2025

Since 1926, the Norwegian American Historical Association's journal *Norwegian-American Studies* has detailed and interpreted the Norwegian-American experience. It remains focused on showcasing new scholarship in the field of Norwegian-American studies, including the related fields of history, literature, religion, art, and cultural studies. The journal aims to not only publish scholarship on Norwegian-American life, but also facilitate intellectual exchange by publishing original research articles alongside discussions of scholarly works in progress, the teaching and learning of Norwegian-American studies, reviews of books recently published in the field, and more.

Norwegian-American Studies (ISSN 0078–1983) is published annually in the fall (Northern Hemisphere) by the University of Minnesota Press and is a benefit of membership in the Norwegian American Historical Association. For current subscription rates please see our website at https://www.upress.umn.edu. Digital subscriptions are available online through the Project MUSE Hosted Journals Program at https://muse.jhu.edu/.

If ordering by mail, please make checks payable to the University of Minnesota Press and send to

Norwegian-American Studies
University of Minnesota Press
111 Third Avenue South, Suite 290
Minneapolis, MN 55401–2520

Address subscription orders, changes of address, and business correspondence (including requests for permission and advertising orders) to the University of Minnesota Press, attention *Norwegian-American Studies.*

Author guidelines and submission preparation materials can be found on the Norwegian American Historical Association website at https://norwegianamerican history.org/norwegian-american-studies/. Direct submissions to the journal editor at editor@norwegianamericanhistory.org.

NAHA Norwegian American Historical Association

The Norwegian American Historical Association (NAHA) is internationally recognized for its major role in furthering the academic study of Norwegian Americans. Since its founding in 1925, NAHA has been dedicated to collecting, preserving, and interpreting the Norwegian-American experience. The NAHA Archives are the largest designated repository for materials about Norwegian-American history and culture in North America. The Association also boasts a robust publications program, including the publication of notable book manuscripts, the academic journal *Norwegian-American Studies,* and a quarterly newsletter. NAHA's work is supported by an active and thriving membership. NAHA is located in the Rolvaag Library on the St. Olaf College campus in Northfield, MN. To learn more, please visit its website at https://norwegianamerican history.org/.

CONTENTS

Norwegian-American Studies 43 • 2025

PHOTOGRAPH FEATURE

The Sámi Reindeer Expedition at Woodland Park in Seattle (1898) as Witnessed Through the Photographs of Anders Beer Wilse

Fred F. Poyner IV

Anders Beer Wilse (1865–1949) was a Norwegian engineer and self-taught photographer who came to America from Norway as a young man, first to Minnesota in 1884 via New York, then to Seattle in 1890. He first found work as a photographer in Washington state with the building of the Great Northern Railway line across Stevens Pass in the Cascade Range. Wilse lived in Seattle between 1892 and 1900. He left a legacy of photographs documenting this period of unprecedented growth and change in Seattle's history.

Figure 1. Anders Beer Wilse and David Kirk, *Untitled* [Sámi reindeer herders of the Lapland-Yukon Relief Expedition, 1898], March 1898 (title assigned by University of Washington Special Collections staff). University of Washington, Special Collections, Wilse no. 388. The expedition numbered 113 men, women, children, and infants. Some of the Sámi families in Washington and Oregon today (particularly those living in Port Angeles and Poulsbo) are descendants of the original herding families.

In that same year, Wilse's engagement of photography as a profession had a profound shift in focus when he joined with travel photographer David Kirk as a business partner to operate a photography studio in Seattle. The commercial success Wilse enjoyed as a result of this enterprise convinced him to remain in the Seattle area and continue documenting subjects that included hotel interiors, the logging industry, Native American encampments, the Klondike gold rush of 1897, and a contingent of visiting Sámi (Saami) reindeer herders to Woodland Park in 1898.

Together with Kirk, the photographer took at least twelve photographs showing a group of 113 Sámi on 8–17 March 1898 during the group's arrival at the downtown train depot and subsequent temporary stay in Woodland Park, Seattle. A collection of these photographs is found today in the Special Collections of the University of Washington.

This group (led by a Norwegian named W. A. Kjellmann) was hired by the US government to shepherd 537 reindeer from Bossekop, Norway, as part of an effort to bring reindeer to the Yup'ik, Iñupiat, and other Arctic Native peoples. While caribou had long been a source of sustenance in the polar regions, some officials in Washington, DC, considered the reindeer imports as serving dual purposes: as a way to promote animal husbandry among those already living there and as a new source of food for the huge influx of gold seekers and others coming to the North.

The transatlantic shipment of this Sámi herd arrived by the steamer *Manitoban* on 24 February 1898 at Jersey City, New Jersey, and the herders were tasked with seeing the herd safely to the West Coast before it took passage on another steamship to the Klondike region of Alaska. The Seattle herd of 1898—or the Yukon Relief Expedition, as it was called at the time—was but one such importation of reindeer of the United States government for the Northern Territories.

Wilse's photographic record provides excellent details about the Sámi, despite their short layover in Seattle to resupply the expedition and arrange passage for the next leg of their journey to the far north. In Wilse photograph number 563, the aforementioned Mr. Kjellmann is pictured holding the tether to a young reindeer calf that has been dehorned. The figure wears a knee-length overcoat,

Figure 2. Anders Beer Wilse and David Kirk, *Kjellman + Young Reindeer Dehorned,* March 1898. University of Washington, Special Collections, Wilse no. 563. The calf shown here was among a total of 537 reindeer that were brought for the expedition, with many that were dehorned for the voyage by land and sea. Kjellmann, a Norwegian from Madison, Wisconsin, grew up working with reindeer in Finnmark County, Norway, and was fluent in the Sámi language. He also supervised the Teller Reindeer Station at Port Clarence, Alaska.

button-down wool jacket, and a square-shaped hat and bears a personage that appears to be one of seriousness, captured in the moment by Wilse's lens. Perhaps Kjellmann was contemplating how to address the many challenges still faced by the group (including the inadvertent loss of the moss that had been packed into the railway cars for the reindeer to eat, discarded by railway porters who believed it was only packing material).

One other individual was named in Wilse's photo series of the Sámi: Samuel Johanesen Balto. The photographer captured a full-length portrait of Balto, similar in style to the other photographs he took of the Sámi, both individually posed and in groups. Balto is shown wearing a heavy fur coat, leggings of fur, boots wrapped with rawhide, and a four-pointed cloth hat (a type of hat called a "Four Winds"). In his right hand, he holds a medal box emblazoned with

Figure 3. Anders Beer Wilse and David Kirk, *Samuel Johanesen Balto That Walked Across Greenland with Nansen,* March 1898. University of Washington, Special Collections, Wilse no. 568. Note the footwear Balto is wearing, called *nutukas,* which are boots made of reindeer hide that are durable protection for cold-weather climates, whether in Kalaallit Nunaat (Greenland) or Alaska. Balto's reputation with Nansen was known to Wilse, and this helped to ensure that Balto's name would be reflected in the photo's title.

a crown; most likely, this is the medal Balto received from the King of Norway, as one of six men who accompanied the Norwegian explorer Fridtjof Nansen across the interior of Greenland in 1888.

Balto originally came from Finnmark County in Norway. The selection and inclusion of many Sámi from the Finnmark region made sense in terms of the expedition's final destination of the cold Alaskan north, as the Finnmark Sámi were reputed as excellent at skiing across vast distances in horrible weather and terrain.

Wilse's visual record of the Sámi in 1898 further illustrates important information about the cultural identity of the group and its members. In a third Wilse photo identified as "number 561," we see a lone Sámi man posed on the top of a railroad car, his right hand tucked inside the fur breast of his coat. Interestingly, the knife sheath he wears on the left side of his belt is shown empty of its blade. Perhaps the man loaned it to another to be used for skinning or to have it sharpened. The timing of the photograph may be concluded by the perspective that it presents: 8 March 1898, owing to the fact that this was the same day that the herd completed its journey to Seattle aboard railroad cars originating from New York.

Figure 4. Anders Beer Wilse and David Kirk, *A Laplander,* March 1898. University of Washington, Special Collections, Wilse no. 561. The long line of boxcars visible behind the Sámi man carried both reindeer and their moss feedstock for the journey to Seattle. Only 185 animals of the 1898 reindeer herd made it to their new moss food source located north of the Chilkat Pass, on the border of Alaska and British Columbia, Canada.

Figure 5. Anders Beer Wilse and David Kirk, *Untitled* [Sámi reindeer herders of the Lapland-Yukon Relief Expedition, probably at Woodland Park, 1898], March 1898 (title assigned by University of Washington Special Collections staff). University of Washington, Special Collections, Wilse no. 573. The Sámi woman carrying the infant with a type of cradleboard known as a *gietkka*. Three other boys visible on the left side of the photo appear to be among the many locals who visited the scene at Woodland Park during the Sámi encampment.

In nine additional Wilse photographs from the 1898 photoshoot, we can observe assembled Sámi in pairs, in a family group of four members, and in larger group portraits numbering between eight and thirty-eight people (e.g., Wilse nos. 557 and 388). The majority of these views show the same clothing style and heavy-duty cold weather materials as those worn by Balto and the second unidentified Sámi man.

Wilse's photographic record was one of many primary sources to document the 1898 reindeer herd. A journal written by one of the Norwegians on the Seattle expedition—*The Yukon Relief Expedition* by Carl Johan Sakariassen—helps to illustrate the origins of the herd and those who tended it. Sakariassen included a copy of the contract of service for the herders, effective 1 February 1898, requiring them "to look out for and take care of reindeer under transport to Alaska . . . [with] a yearly salary of Kr.1000 (one thousand crowns) with good and sufficient food and clothes (tobacco not included) and free transport to Alaska."[1] In Figure 5, we see a group of Sámi that includes two men, a young child, and a woman carrying an infant; this reflects the broad range of ages of the expedition's members, which included extended families. In the distant background, several articles of clothing are seen spread out on park foliage to airdry in the sun.

While the story of the Sámi who accompanied the reindeer to Seattle in 1898 was only partially told through Wilse's photographs, his contribution to the visual record was important nonetheless for the details these images, on their own and collectively, offer as insight into the identity of the group and the work they performed. These Sámi photographs are all the more valuable to the historical record, considering that Wilse himself did not describe this as a photo series in volume 1 of his autobiography *En Emigrants Ungdomserindringer* (Life of a Norwegian pioneer), first published in 1936.[2]

Fred F. Poyner IV *is an independent historian and author who enjoys researching and writing about the art and history of the Pacific Northwest, including public sculpture. He is currently a grant writer for the Sauk-Suiattle Indian Tribe (Sah-ku-méhu) in Washington state and a regular contributor to* The Filson Journal *since 2019. His latest book is* Native American and First Nation Figures in Sculpture: North American Monuments, Memorials and Statuary of 50 Artists.

NOTES

This photograph feature is an excerpt from a presentation offered at "Nordic Immigration in the Pacific Northwest, from Then to Now: Technology, Innovation, and Migration," hosted by the National Nordic Museum in Seattle, Washington (2016).

1. Carl Johan Sakariassen, V. R. Rausch, and D. L. Baldwin, eds., *The Yukon Relief Expedition and the Journal of Carl Johan Sakariassen* (University of Alaska Press, 2002), 35.
2. Anders Beer Wilse, *Anders Beer Wilse Photography: Life of a Young Norwegian Pioneer / En Emigrants Ungdomserindringer,* vol. 1, ed. Deb Nelson Gourley and Christian Wilse (1936; Astri My Astri Publishing, 2015).

WORKS IN PROGRESS

A Roundtable Discussion of the State of the Field of Norwegian-American Studies

Terje Mikael Hasle Joranger, Lori Ann Lahlum, Odd S. Lovoll, Inger Marie Okkenhaug, Caitlin Sackrison, and Anna M. Peterson

ANNA M. PETERSON (AP). What is one of the articles or books written in the field of Norwegian-American studies that has been most influential in your own work? How has it shaped your understanding of the Norwegian-American experience?

ODD S. LOVOLL (OL). Ingrid Semmingsen, *Veien mot vest. Utvandringen fra Norge til Amerika 1825–1865* (1941) and *Utvandringen fra Norge 1865–1915* (1950). Semmingsen's body of work is a Norwegian national treasure. How to best write the history of Norwegians who emigrated and their relationship with the homeland was much discussed and debated from the early 1900s.

It was finally achieved and resolved with Semmingsen's two pioneer volumes. Her focus is worldwide, but most of the history covers Norwegians in America. Semmingsen makes Norwegian Americans an integrated part of Norwegian history. Norwegians were finally accepted by the homeland as genuine Norwegians. Semmingsen discusses Norwegian social history in the nineteenth century. As I perused her account of emigration, its causes, the adversity individual immigrants experienced, and their adjustment to a foreign land, I saw my own immigrant experience. She became my primary inspiration as I established myself as an authority in the field of Norwegian immigration. Her major works with their strong humanistic and social historical perspectives will remain as classic interpretations of Norwegian emigration history and make immigration history scholarly, interesting, and popular.

TERJE MIKAEL HASLE JORANGER (TJ). In his monograph *The Minds of the West: Ethnocultural Evolution in the Rural Middle West, 1830–1917* (1997), Jon Gjerde studies the "minds" or cultural patterns among immigrant groups in the Middle West. He emphasizes that cultural transplantation took place due to the patterns of migration that reunited people of similar pasts. Besides, he treats the rural Midwest as a region where immigrant groups could build tight-knit settlements and segregate themselves from other cultural groups. Gjerde makes comparisons between patterns of development and acculturation across immigrant groups. He also explores frictions within and between communities and how various ethnic groups portrayed their characteristics in political and social debate regionally and nationally.

Gjerde's study helped lift the Norwegian-American experience from a tradition of methodological nationalism that characterized Norwegian-American studies from the early publications in the field. By studying the interplay between Norwegians and several other ethnic groups, Gjerde's study helps broaden the perspective from a large focus on the development of the Norwegian immigrant group in its own right. I think that it is by studying the dynamics between various ethnic groups and comparing these characteristics that we can find out more about inherent characteristics among each group and to which extent the dynamics between the various ethnic groups create change among these groups.

INGER MARIE OKKENHAUG (IO). Similar to Terje, I find that Jon Gjerde's impressive study *The Minds of the West: Ethnocultural Evolution in the Rural Middle West, 1830–1917* has been influential in several ways: Gjerde includes a gendered perspective on immigrant family structures and life stories. He shows how Norwegian-American farmers were part of the "European-American" family structure, keeping the patriarchal family arrangement of the old country. Many male heads of Norwegian households often increased their authority due to frontier conditions. At the same time, these men and their wives had to adjust to a modern agricultural society that was money-based to a much higher degree than Norwegian rural society. Thus, Gjerde's characterization of Norwegian immigration culture as a unique culture, a hybrid of Norwegian and American cultures, has been important in my understanding of the Norwegian-American experience.

LORI ANN LAHLUM (LL). The book that has had the greatest impact on my work and understanding of Norwegian America is Jon Gjerde's *From Peasants to Farmers: The Migration from Norway to the Upper Middle West* (1985). I read *From Peasants to Farmers* during the first year of my PhD program. As I began work on an American environmental history paper about Norwegian immigrant women, landscape, and agriculture, *From Peasants to Farmers* helped me contextualize what I had found in primary sources. When I began my PhD program, the intersection of gender, environment, and agriculture wasn't going to be my dissertation topic. After reading my paper, W. R. Swagerty, my adviser and professor for the course, told me he thought this should be my dissertation project, and I embraced this line of inquiry. Later, Gjerde's work made me realize that understanding the Norwegian context would be crucial for my work as well, which fundamentally reframed how I approached the dissertation.

L. DeAne Lagerquist's book on women and gender in Norwegian American (*In America the Men Milk the Cows: Factors of Gender, Ethnicity, and Religion in the Americanization of Norwegian-American Women* [1991]) has also profoundly impacted my work. When I started research on my dissertation, there was very little scholarship on Norwegian immigrant women or gender in Norwegian-American communities. Yes, there were many books and articles that included collections of Norwegian immigrant women's letters or diaries, but there was a scholarly void. *In America the Men Milk the Cows* was pioneering in that regard.

CAITLIN SACKRISON (CS). For my own work on Norwegian-American homesteading women in Minnesota, the most influential book has been Karen V. Hansen's *Encounter on the Great Plains: Scandinavian Settlers and the Dispossession of Dakota Indians, 1890–1930* (2013). While this book has shifted many conversations in Norwegian-American history surrounding the role of Norwegian immigrants in Indigenous displacement and dispossession, it was also the demographic work and analysis of Karen V. Hansen that has inspired how I find and examine Norwegian-American women. It must be noted that Karen V. Hansen was also my adviser, and the primary reason why I pursued Norwegian-American history for my PhD, so her book, coupled with her outside knowledge, was incredibly influential for my own research. As a descendant of Norwegian immigrants to America, *Encounter on the Great Plains* challenged me to consider the many layers of history in the nineteenth century. Initially, I was primarily interested in learning more about Norwegian-American women's rights and resilience, but I also had to understand the legacy of settler colonialism and Dakota dispossession to fully understand how many Norwegian immigrants, including my family, were able to settle and thrive on land that was not uninhabited but had been the homeland of Indigenous Americans.

AP. If someone asked you to recommend an introductory text to the field, which text would you recommend and why?

IO. Nils Olav Østrem's short but thoroughly researched *Norsk utvandringshistorie* (2014) deals with both reasons for the emigration and the migrants' experiences in North America and gives an excellent overview of the history and historiography of Norwegian migration. Østrem has, however, been criticized for not including the dispossession of the Native Americans in his book. For that reason, in addition to *Norsk utvandringshistorie,* I would recommend Karen V. Hansen's introduction in her book *Encounter on the Great Plains: Scandinavian Settlers and the Dispossession of Dakota Indians, 1890–1930.* Hansen's focus is on Norwegian migrants as land-takers and the colonial aspect of Scandinavian migration in American history.

OL. Marcus Lee Hansen, "Immigration as a Field for Historical Research," *American Historical Review* 32 (1927): 500–18. Marcus Lee Hansen's article makes a meaningful investigation of migration acceptable as scholarly subject matter. It establishes Hansen as "the father of modern historical scholarship in migration." He served on the Norwegian American Historical Association's board of editors and influenced its publications. His listed reasons for the study of migration are valuable contributions to the field. Rudolph J. Vecoli, "*Contadini* in Chicago: A Critique of *The Uprooted,*" *Journal of American History* 51, no. 3 (1964): 405–17. Rudolph J. Vecoli's article published in 1964 changed the field of immigration history in the United States. Vecoli takes exception to the immigration classic *The Uprooted: The Epic Story of the Great Migrations That Made the American People* (1951) and challenges its distinguished author Oscar Handlin, who writes within the assimilationist scholarly tradition. Instead of assimilating quickly, Vecoli argues, the Italian *contadini*—peasant farmers—"clung tenaciously to their traditions and developed strategies to retain their heritage." Vecoli was my mentor for my doctoral degree on the Norwegian-American *bygdelag.* Like the *contadini,* they embraced their local Norwegian heritage. I owe much to Vecoli also in my later scholarly works.

LL. For a broad overview of the Norwegian-American experience, one should look at Odd S. Lovoll's *The Promise of America: A History of the Norwegian-American People* (1984) because of its breadth and accessibility. I'd like to mention a couple of other books that are engaging and accessible. For example, Kathleen Stokker's *Remedies and Rituals: Folk Medicine in Norway and the New Land* (2007) does a wonderful job connecting medical practices and traditions in Norway and Norwegian-American communities. It's also thought-provoking. Finally, *Colonel Hans Christian Heg and the Norwegian American Experience* (2023) by Odd S. Lovoll provides a good introduction to Norwegian settler communities in Wisconsin, Norwegian-American politics, and Norwegian Americans and the Civil War.

CS. Since many of the people I talk to about Norwegian-American history are interested in learning more about Norwegian immigrant women in America, I always point readers to Betty A. Bergland and Lori Ann Lahlum's *Norwegian American Women: Migration, Communities, and Identities* (2011). I find the various series of essays in *Norwegian American Women* often provide readers with a point of entry into the history they are looking for. I also find that many readers end up reading the entire book and learn not only about Norwegian-American women but also about all of the spaces in society, culture, and the economy that women have been part of in history. While many readers are used to seeing history books that are focused on political or military history, I find social and cultural history is often less understood. *Norwegian American Women* uses cultural and social history to remind readers that those are distinct spaces where we can see women exercise authority, shaping history and culture in ways that continue to impact many of us today.

TJ. I would recommend Orm Øverland's prologue to his book *Immigrant Minds, American Identities: Making the United States Home, 1870–1930* (2000). Øverland defines homemaking myths as "particular constructions of ethnic memory to ensure and improve an ethnic as well as an American future." These myths focus on a specific group's right to a home in America. Furthermore, Øverland asserts that homemaking myths should be considered an essential feature of American ethnicity in the last decades of the nineteenth century and the first decades of the twentieth century.

The prologue to *Immigrant Minds, American Identities* explores contexts and expressions of observers among Norwegian Americans and other ethnic groups of the view that they were the best Americans due to their specific national traits and traditions. The author discusses how homemaking myths during the period in question were not only a Norwegian-American phenomenon but also a general trait among several ethnic groups. I would assert that the topic is not only relevant for the time period 1870–1930 but also highly relevant to contemporary readers. Global and transnational migrations are still prevalent. Furthermore, the inclusion of the Norwegian-American experience in larger historical contexts is concrete and meaningful in that it grapples with general processes of identity formation in immigrant groups.

AP. What excites you most about the work currently being done in the field of Norwegian-American studies?

LL. I'm excited about the work being done on settler colonialism and race in Norwegian America. Norwegian-American history has lagged behind in terms of tackling these pressing topics. It's wonderful to see so much work being done in the past few years. Of course, there are people, like Betty A. Bergland, who have grappled with these topics for more than twenty-five years, but much of the work is more recent.

TJ. Norwegian-American studies makes up part of a larger historical context that takes into account the continuous linkages between local communities, regions, and the national level in the United States and Norway. The focus on transnational history is partly based on digitization and the availability of new online resources. For example, the larger availability of Norwegian and Norwegian-American newspapers and archival collections in museums and historical societies makes Norwegian-American studies more accessible for scholars and for those interested in Norwegian-American studies. The availability of new source material forms a basis for disciplinary and interdisciplinary studies in the field.

IO. I am motivated by the study of Norwegian immigration to North American cities, giving insights to the urban migration experience—for example, David C. Mauk's recent book *The Heart of the Heartland: Norwegian American Community in the Twin Cities* (2022).

OL. I am excited to see the persistent interest in Norwegian-American history. As an example, I can relate my own experience in Norway. On 6 July 2023, I spoke to a full auditorium at the University of Oslo about my recent publication *Colonel Hans Christian Heg and the Norwegian American Experience.* The people present showed much interest in the topic. I am now advising a person who was inspired by my talk to add a doctoral degree in history to his earlier degree in law. He is comparing the experience of Norwegian settlers in North Dakota with the German Russians in the same state.

CS. In the past decade, there has been a turn toward cultural, social, and revisionist history in many recently published Norwegian-American history articles and books. From Anders Bo Rasmussen's *Civil War Settlers: Scandinavians, Citizenship, and American Empire, 1848–1870* (2022) to *Nordic Whiteness and Migration to the USA: A Historical Exploration of Identity,* edited by Jana Sverdljuk, Terje Mikael Hasle Joranger, Erika K. Jackson, and Peter Kivisto (2021), there have been many scholars looking to reexamine and elaborate on Norwegian-American ideology and action surrounding topics like race, colonization, and gender. As many areas of American history are being reexamined, it is exciting to see Norwegian-American history moving in this direction too, since it provides us with a more accurate understanding of Norwegian-American history and helps us better appreciate the lives of historically marginalized people in America.

AP. Where do you hope to see the field going in the future?

CS. Norwegian-American studies has historically been of interest to Norwegian Americans, yet many Americans feel less tied to their Norwegian heritage due to generational shifts and distance between those who immigrated to America and their modern-day descendants. Many

Americans are also proud of multiple identities, whether that is tied with another immigrant group or another community that they are connected to. With that in mind, I hope the field embraces those who may not identify as Norwegian-American or who possess many different identities including Norwegian-American, as their perspectives can provide insight into new topics related to Norwegian-American studies. These new insights may also keep this field relevant for more modern audiences. I also hope that we embrace more mediums for sharing this history, as that might encourage more people to contribute to the field in new and innovative ways.

IO. I would like to see more research on return migrants. Between 1/4 and 1/3 of all migrants returned to Norway (including several of my foremothers and -fathers) and influenced the modernization processes in Norway in many-faceted ways. In addition, the personal aspect: Life stories of return migrants is an understudied theme. To develop the field using tools from the "history of emotions" would be fruitful to gain a deeper understanding of the migrant experience.

OL. I certainly hope that the scholarly and general history of migration will continue. There will be a more inclusive ethnic history and less of an isolated national story as most American citizens will have several ethnic heritages to observe.

TJ. I hope that the field will broaden its traditional basis on Norwegian migration to the United States into a wider thematic, temporal, and spatial focus. In terms of a thematic focus, I'd like to see more narratives about Norwegian immigrants and their interactions with other ethnic groups, including Indigenous populations, African Americans, and Sámi immigrants to North America.[1]

I'd also like to see a broader temporal focus that includes Norwegian emigration prior to 1825 and after 1925, such as studies of Norwegian emigration to the Netherlands and subsequent emigration to the Dutch colonies in North America in the seventeenth century and to Dano-Norwegian colonies in the Caribbean in the eighteenth century.

Norwegian-American studies should naturally include Canada as well. A far larger population from Norway immigrated to the United States than to Canada, but the migration patterns between the two countries are interlinked and should be studied more in tandem than has been done earlier.

LL. I hope scholars continue to address issues of race and gender in settler communities. My concern is that many (and probably most) of the scholars who work in Norwegian-American history consider themselves first and foremost a scholar of something else, and I'm one of these people. My dissertation was on Norwegian-American history, and I've published largely in Norwegian-American history, yet my adviser and program were outside of the field. To sustain the field in a meaningful kind of way, there needs to be an investment at a PhD-granting institution. Sadly, I don't see that happening. While the field may not have institutional support, one of the great strengths is that there is an active, engaged, and knowledgeable lay population. The commitment by laypeople to the field ensures its success. They enrich our conferences and are largely responsible for the popularity of our books. I hope this collaboration continues as our field grows and changes.

***Terje Mikael Hasle Joranger** is research director at the Norwegian Emigrant Museum and professor in history at the University of Inland Norway in Hamar. He is professionally responsible for Crossings 200 in Norway and is editor of* Norwegian-American Essays *published by NAHA-Norway.*

***Lori Ann Lahlum** recently retired from Minnesota State University, Mankato. She and Betty A. Bergland coedited* Norwegian American Women: Migration, Communities, and Identities. *In 2019, the South Dakota Historical Society Press released* Equality at the Ballot Box: Votes for Women on the Northern Great Plains, *a book Lahlum coedited with Molly P. Rozum.*

***Odd S. Lovoll** received his education both in Norway and the United States, earning a PhD in United States history in 1973 with a specialization in immigration. He served thirty years on the faculty of St. Olaf College, retiring from the King Olav V Chair in*

Scandinavian-American Studies at the end of 2000. From 1996 to 2005, he served as adjunct professor (professor II) of history at the University of Oslo, and from 1980 to 2001 he served as NAHA's publications editor. His most recent book on the Norwegian-American immigrant experience is titled Colonel Hans Christian Heg and the Norwegian American Experience.

Inger Marie Okkenhaug *is professor at the Department of History, Volda University College. Her recent publications include "Transitions, Transformations and Contact Zones: Sibling Migration to Minnesota, 1881–1891," in* Kontaktsoner og grenseområder, *ed. Chalak Kaveh, Harald Endre Tafjord, and Ola Teige (2023) and* Historien om Palestina og Israel i moderne tid *(A modern history of Palestine and Israel), coauthored with Jens Johan Hyvik (2024).*

Caitlin Sackrison *is visiting assistant professor of Norwegian at St. Olaf College. Her teaching and research focus on immigration history, women's history, and gender and sexuality studies with a geographical focus on European, Nordic, and American spaces.*

Anna M. Peterson *is associate professor of history at Luther College in Decorah, IA. She also serves as editor for the Norwegian American Historical Association. Her publications in the field of Norwegian-American studies have focused on the intersections of Norwegian immigration, ethnic identity formation, and the woman suffrage movement as well as most recently the Native American experiences at the Norwegian-American-run Bethany Indian Mission.*

NOTE

1. Mary Louise Pratt's concept of "contact zones" is relevant in this regard. The concept is used to define "social spaces where cultures meet, clash, and grapple with each other, often in contexts of highly asymmetrical relations of power." Mary Louise Pratt, *Imperial Eyes: Travel Writing and Transculturation,* 2nd ed. (Routledge, 2008), 34.

Pastor Claus L. Clausen's Backstage Biography

Jostein Garcia de Presno

Introduction

Pastor Claus L. Clausen (1820–1892), originally from Denmark, features in practically every account of early Norwegian immigration to the United States. His varied career continues to fascinate Norwegian-American historiography even today.[1] This is hardly surprising. Shortly after immigrating in 1843, Clausen became the pastor of the first Norwegian congregation to be organized in America, in the Muskego settlement in the territory of Wisconsin. For the next forty-odd years, he served Norwegian immigrants in a multitude of ways and in ever-new locations. In the course of his impressive career, he founded twenty congregations, initiated two journals, founded two synods, led a company of settlers to found the town of Saint Ansgar in Iowa, and served as a chaplain during the Civil War, to name but a few of his many accomplishments. The church historian I. A. Bergh argued that, for all intents and purposes, Clausen must be reckoned as a

Figure 1. Framed portrait of Claus L. Clausen, date unknown. Original at Vesterheim Norwegian-American Museum in Decorah, Iowa. Photograph by Jostein Garcia de Presno.

Norwegian pastor, as "all his clerical work was performed among and for Norwegians."[2] Although Danes might not agree with this logic, it should be reason enough for revisiting one of the protagonists of the pioneer days of Norwegian immigration in connection with this year's commemoration.

This study does not focus on Clausen's numerous achievements in the United States, however. Instead, it aims to accomplish two goals. The first goal is to shed new light on the events that led to Clausen's decision to emigrate. This article includes an English translation of one of Clausen's early letters, which until now has remained unknown to American scholarship. In the letter, young Clausen recounts to a Danish friend, Ludvig Hass, in quite some detail, events of his youth and his many efforts to become a missionary. The account greatly expands our understanding of Clausen's youth and of the push-and-pull factors that eventually led him to choose America over Africa. Interestingly, this account from young Clausen differs in significant ways from an autobiography that he composed in his old age. As becomes evident when comparing the two accounts, several events from Clausen's youth have either been glossed over or altered in the narrative given by the older Clausen. The second goal of this article is therefore to discuss the key discrepancies between the two accounts and what they can tell us about Clausen's self-presentation as a retired pastor in Minnesota. What follows is first the discussion of the two accounts, after which Clausen's letter to Hass is rendered.

The Frontstage and Backstage of Immigrant Lives

Self-presentations are a well-known phenomenon in immigration sources, so Clausen's two self-presentations are in good company. The sociologist Erving Goffman coined the terms *frontstage* and *backstage* to refer to social regions that require different kinds of self-presentation. Simply speaking, frontstage is where a performance is presented, and backstage is where it is prepared. Importantly, the backstage is not to be shown to the audience. However, the boundaries between frontstage and backstage can sometimes be blurred. A frontstage presentation to an earlier audience may, for instance, be inconsistent with expectations among a later audience. What was once a frontstage presentation may thus become an inconvenient backstage to the present. As a consequence, a past presentation might be considered to contain "dark secrets" that are incompatible with a self-presentation that someone currently wishes to maintain.

As any autobiography is a self-presentation, Goffman's concepts of frontstage and backstage are well suited for discussing Clausen's two autobiographical accounts. Young Clausen's account, which he wrote in the abovementioned letter to Hass, was, at the time of writing, a frontstage presentation. The intended audience was the radical Danish revivalist community of which Clausen was a part at that time. However, after a lifelong pastoral career in the United States, the retired Clausen had gained a new audience when composing his autobiography—namely, his Norwegian-American congregations. The two self-presentations, therefore, had quite different audiences in mind. In other words, Clausen's former frontstage presentation was in several ways at odds with his new pastoral role and had become backstage to his current life in the United States. Consequently, Clausen's autobiography from his retirement in Minnesota came to be quite different from his former self-presentation.

The Retired Clausen's Frontstage Autobiography

According to Clausen's autobiography, which he composed during his retirement, he was born on the island of Ærø in Denmark, and his parents were "honorable Christian people."[3] The young Claus had poor health, but he was quick to learn and had a good memory. Although he did not get along with the local pastor, he did well during confirmation. Afterward, he was placed by his father as an apprentice at an estate manager's office on the neighboring island of Fyn, with the intention of proceeding to study law. However, while on Fyn, Clausen was awakened through contact with a childhood friend. This planted in him a growing desire to become a missionary. When he returned to Ærø, the new pastor there recognized Clausen's intellectual potential. They made an agreement that Clausen would undertake to tutor the pastor's children in exchange for private theological instruction. After some time with this arrangement, the pastor believed that Clausen was ready to study theology. Unfortunately, it was impossible for Clausen to pursue this course of action due to "lack of necessary funds."[4]

Instead of going to Copenhagen to study theology, Clausen took a position as a tutor on the neighboring island of Langeland. Unfortunately, he soon had to abandon this job, as he "could not tolerate the sedentary life" of teaching. His doctor therefore advised him "to take a long walking tour in Norway or Switzerland."[5] Having read a lot about the Norwegian revivalist Hans Nielsen Hauge's travels, which had greatly interested him, he decided on Norway. In 1841, he traveled around Norway, becoming acquainted with many Haugians along the way, among them Tollef Bache. He also met pastor W. A. Wexels and Andreas Hauge (the son of Hans Nielsen Hauge) in Oslo (Christiania).

Upon returning home to Denmark, Clausen received an inquiry from Hauge and Wexels in Oslo, asking if he would consider being the assistant of Hans Schreuder, who was soon to depart as Norwegian missionary to South Africa. Clausen returned to Norway the following year, this time to discuss his options for joining Schreuder. During the discussions, obstacles to his missionary plans soon arose, specifically regarding the possibilities for Clausen himself to be ordained. If Schreuder were to die, "Clausen would be left alone in the heathen lands among a foreign people, and as long as he was not ordained, it would be practically impossible for him to accomplish anything under such circumstances."[6]

Clausen went on to inquire both in Denmark and Norway about the possibilities for being ordained when sent out as a missionary. While waiting for a response, he received an inquiry from Norwegian immigrants in Muskego, Wisconsin, via his Haugian friend Bache, asking if he would consider going to America to become a teacher for Norwegian immigrant children instead and eventually "to become their pastor." Clausen now came to the conviction "that his true calling was to the Scandinavians in America rather than going out among the heathen. He therefore decided, in Jesus' name, to follow the calling to America."[7] Thus, Clausen emigrated to work as a teacher among Norwegians in the United States instead of becoming a missionary to South Africa. Soon after his arrival in Muskego, he was ordained, and the rest is Norwegian-Danish-American immigration history.

Pastoral and Personal Troubles

Clausen's frontstage presentation from his retirement in Minnesota certainly made a good fit with his lifelong career as a pastor. If we pause for a moment to consider the reason why he wrote it, it may very well have been that he was anxious what the narrative about the unschooled Danish pioneer pastor might look like if schooled Norwegian theologians were to author it. Anyone familiar with Clausen's story will know that his life in the United States had consisted of more than accomplishments. As a pastor he was also highly contested, and his main critics were none other than his colleagues in the Norwegian Synod. Some of the controversies that surrounded him can be useful for understanding the differences between his self-presentations and the way in which the retired Clausen later framed his road to emigration. There were three particular things about Clausen that aggravated the other pastors.

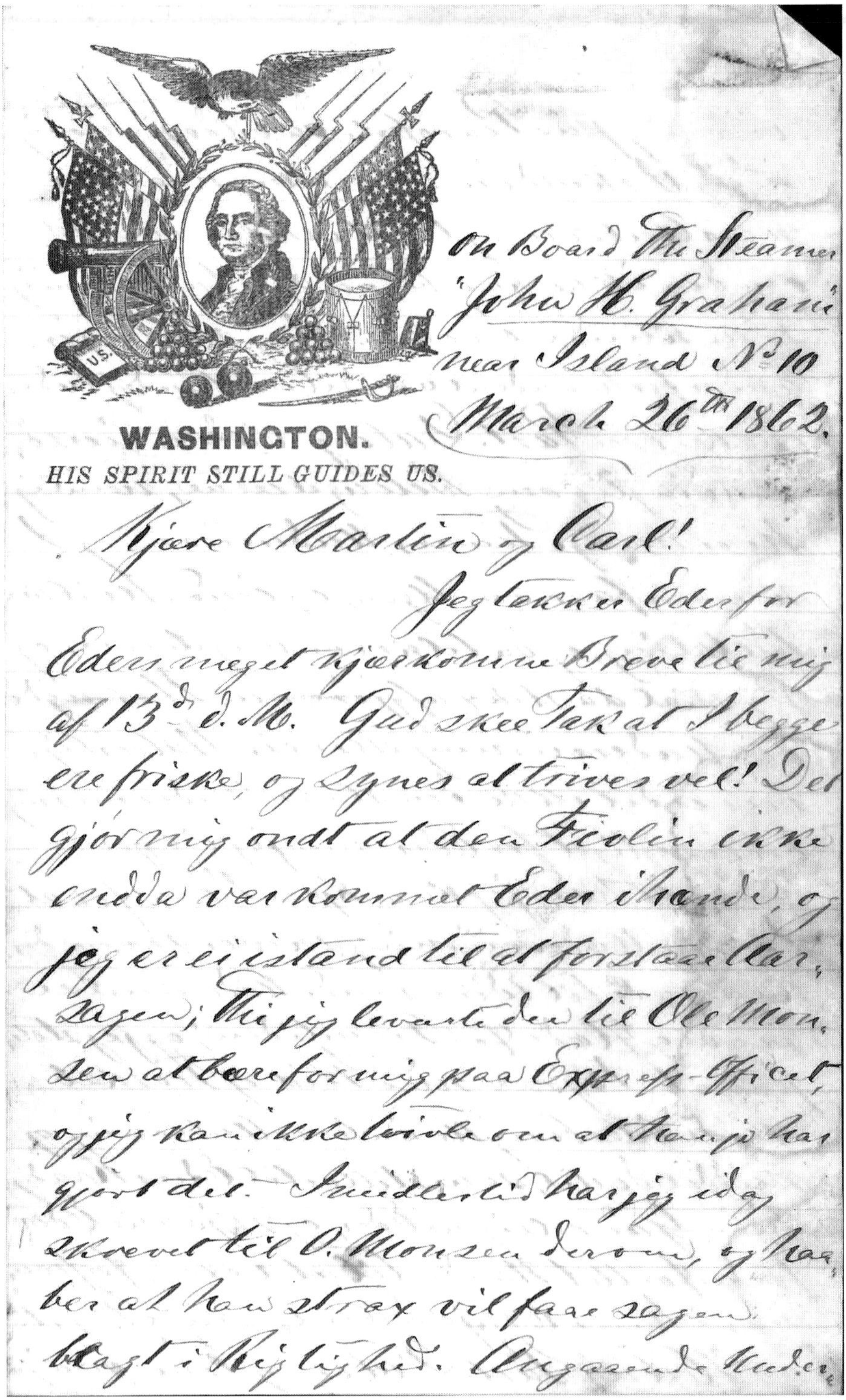

WASHINGTON.
HIS SPIRIT STILL GUIDES US.

On Board The Steamer
"John H. Graham"
near Island No 10
March 26th 1862.

Kjære Martin og Carl!

Jeg takker Eder for Eders meget kjærkomne Breve til mig af 13de d. M. Gud skee Tak at I begge ere friske, og synes at trives vel! Det gjør mig ondt at den Fiolin ikke endda var kommet Eder ihænde, og jeg er ei istand til at forstaae Aarsagen; thi jeg leverte den til Ole Monsen at bære for mig paa Express-Officet, og jeg kan ikke tvivle om at han jo har gjort det. Imidlertid har jeg idag skrevet til O. Monsen derom, og har bet at han strax vil faae sagen bragt i Rigtighed. Angaaende Under-

Figure 2. The first page of a letter from Clausen to his two eldest sons, Martin and Carl, when he was serving as chaplain in the Scandinavian Regiment during the Civil War. Original at RG 15, Papers of Claus L. Clausen, Luther College Archives, Luther College. Photograph by Jostein Garcia de Presno.

First, Clausen was repeatedly at odds with them regarding theological issues. Best known is his principled stance against slavery, which spurred a debate within the Norwegian community that was to last almost a decade.[8] Another issue, more pertinent to the current discussion, was Clausen's subscription to the theology of the Danish pastor N. F. S. Grundtvig (1783–1872).[9] One main point of argument was whether Christian baptism and the Apostles' Creed could be traced back to Jesus independently of the authority of the New Testament.[10] Leaning on Grundtvig, Clausen claimed that it could; the rest of the pastors firmly rejected the idea. Later, after having been out of pastoral service for a few years, when Clausen asked to be taken up again as a member of the Norwegian Synod, he was readmitted only on condition that he "repent" from his Grundtvigian "heresies."[11] This he subsequently did, as always overly conscious about his own lack of formal theological training.[12]

Second, there was the matter of Clausen's health. Although his poor health was well known, there was an impression among the other pastors that "health problems" sometimes served as a convenient excuse for covering over other reasons that caused Clausen to pull out and move on.[13] Several times, for instance, he withdrew completely from pastoral service allegedly due to poor health at times that happened to coincide with bitter controversies. When this happened yet again in 1876, the editor of a journal with which Clausen had a long history of conflict commented sarcastically that this had now occurred so many times that even Clausen must have lost count.[14]

Third, nothing annoyed the other pastors more than their experience that Clausen would change his mind to suit his purposes. This was claimed several times during the confrontations with Clausen in the slavery debate. In their opinion, he was also often outright untruthful about the past.[15] Accusations about Clausen's unsteadiness and untrustworthiness did not only come from colleagues. Søren Bache, a fellow pioneer settler in Muskego, had accused Clausen of the same tendency already in the early years of the settlement.[16] Interestingly, the letter at the end of this article was written by Clausen precisely as a reply to accusations from his friend Hass about wavering and fickleness. These three accusations, then—Grundtvigianism, alleged health issues, and fickleness—were repeatedly raised against Clausen during his career.

Backstage Secrets

Although not all this smoke may have been entirely well grounded, there certainly seems to have been some fire to cause it. If we assume that the pastors' complaints had some substance to them, what might we expect to find if we take a closer look at Clausen's autobiography? For one thing, we may suspect Clausen of not having been entirely truthful about past events or having presented them in such a way as to suit later purposes. Further, Clausen might be expected to have blamed his health at some point or other for a decision to move or break up. Finally, he probably was not too keen to highlight his past Grundtvigian beliefs too much.

Rather interestingly, these hypothetical expectations all find resonance when comparing Clausen's old-age autobiography with sources from his younger years in Denmark. Some of this will be evident simply from reading his letter to Hass. Other parts need a little more explanation. What follows is a discussion of what we might call five "backstage secrets" from Clausen's past that emerge from a comparison of the two autobiographical accounts. While they all play a significant part in his early account, they are all but gone from his old-age autobiography. They have to do with painful familial relations, Clausen's anticlericalism, a Grundtvigian mission trip to Norway, Clausen's insistence on ordination, and his engagement to Martha. As will become clear, some of these matters he simply left out when writing his autobiography in Minnesota. Others he framed into a more convenient presentation.

Conflicts in the Clausen Family

The first issue, and one that Clausen left out altogether from this autobiography, was the troubled relationship that he on several occasions had with his parents, particularly his father. The reason for the familial clashes was Clausen's participation in the local revival on Ærø after his return from Fyn. An important background for his participation is another point that Clausen later failed to mention but that is crucial for understanding the course of events. Significantly, Clausen's awakening on Fyn was not at all an isolated event. It was, in fact, part of a nationwide, radical Danish revival in the 1830s, spreading across the country precisely from Fyn.[17] It consisted mostly in laypeople conducting religious assemblies, so-called conventicles, in violation of the Conventicle Act.[18] In fact, the most active speaker in the conventicles on the island of Ærø was none other than Clausen.[19]

As Clausen relates in the letter to Hass below, he was actually kicked out of his home three times by his own father as a result of his participation in the revival. To begin with, Clausen's revival activities annoyed the whole family. But quite soon his sister was awakened, and then his mother too. This aggravated his father tremendously, who found no better reaction than to kick young Claus out. The expulsion only contributed to increasing Clausen's engagement with the revival, however, and eventually led him to move to the neighboring island of Langeland and join the revivalists there. In that way, the expulsions actually made a significant contribution to Clausen's eventual decision to emigrate. It was due to being forced to leave home that he seriously started to consider becoming a missionary, and it was on Langeland that he made the acquaintances that eventually would bring him to America.

The troubled family relationships of his youth were extremely painful for Clausen to dwell on later in life. This must have been one of the reasons for altogether leaving them out of his later autobiography. Another reason was probably that his family, even his father, all eventually seem to have joined the revival.[20] Looking back, Clausen described his parents as "honorable Christian people" and his move to Langeland as motivated by taking up tutoring there.[21] This was not wholly untrue, but it certainly was not the whole story.

Clausen's Anticlericalism

Second, the Danish revival of the 1830s was largely anticlerical. In the eyes of many a revivalist, the academic study of theology was the opposite of true Christianity. Laypeople accused pastors of lacking a true Christian spirit, and pastors accused revivalists of fanaticism. Clausen was no exception to this general picture; in fact, he was one of the harshest critics of pastors of the state church. While on Ærø, he even wrote a hymn about pastoral vices, one of the verses of which goes like this:

> The country teems with so-called pastors,
> Who ought to preach the word of truth,
> But alas, most are like their master,
> The devil, full of lies and murder,
> Virtues and deeds are their teaching,
> The grace in Christ is silenced,
> Burdens of the law for the people to carry,
> The pastor himself never carries a feather.[22]

Understandably, there is no mention of this hostile attitude to pastors in Clausen's autobiography. After all, after immigrating he went on to become a prominent pastor among Norwegian Americans. As a pastor in the Norwegian Synod, he also had many a conflict with the more anticlerical Elling Eielsen (1804–1883) and the Norwegian Haugians.[23] It simply would not have done to have them holding his own past against him.

Clausen did not only leave out his past anticlerical views from his autobiography; he also modified the portrayal of a significant event that came precisely as a result of his anticlericalism. According to the autobiography, Clausen could not proceed to study theology due to a "lack of necessary funds." In the letter to Hass, however, a wholly different explanation is given. Clausen explains that his father was more than willing to pay for his theological studies. It was even his father's initiative that Clausen should become a pastor in the first place. The reason Claus did not concede was rather his distrust of academic theology. He was genuinely concerned about losing his own awakened faith were he to enroll at the University of Copenhagen. "Who could guarantee that my spiritual life would not be lost if I went to the ungodly university, and my occupation mostly consisted of philosophical ponderings?" he wonders in the letter to Hass.[24] So the reason Clausen did not study theology did not have anything to do with his financial status. It was a decision of his own choice, based on his strong, anticlerical attitude.

Baptists and Grundtvigian Mission

Third, in Clausen's autobiography there is nothing to explain why Clausen, in the United States, proved such a strong believer in the Grundtvigian doctrine of baptism. His Grundtvigian convictions are not mentioned at all. As a matter of fact, it was precisely due to the theology of Grundtvig that Clausen went from being anticlerical to seeking ordination. Furthermore, Grundtvig's views on baptism had played a significant role in Clausen's life on a very personal level and had greatly influenced his decision to emigrate. This helps explain why Clausen found it so painful later in life to distance himself from this teaching.

Just about when Clausen was being kicked out from home for the third time, Baptists from Germany started entering Denmark.[25] Although their missionary activity was strictly illegal in the Evangelical-Lutheran monarchy, many of the revivalists were attracted to their message. Clausen was one of those who for a time considered being baptized by them.[26] His flirtation with Baptism lasted only a few months, however, and the reason it passed so quickly is important. It was precisely due to the influence of Grundtvig-inspired pastors and eventually a meeting with Grundtvig himself that Clausen ended up rejecting the teaching of the Baptists. Through Grundtvig's teaching that Jesus's command to baptize was earlier than, and independent of, the New Testament, Clausen was assured that he had already received the grace of God when he was baptized as a child. Consequently, living a Christian life was about finding a way back to and relying on the "Covenant of Baptism," which was already granted him by God, not about conversion and needing to be baptized again.

So consequential were Grundtvig's teachings about baptism for Clausen, that he decided to leave Langeland and go on a mission trip to Norway to preach this message to Norwegian revivalists, the Haugians.[27] According to Clausen's autobiography, the trip to Norway was for health purposes and, as such, could equally well have been to Switzerland. As the letter to Hass describes in detail, however, the reasons were much more complex, had nothing to do with Clausen's health, and even involved yet another trip to Norway.

As mentioned in his autobiography, for several years Clausen had been dreaming of going away to "the heathen" as a missionary. In the letter to Hass, we are told that he had even secretly planned to enlist as crew on a ship, only to be able to steal away when the ship was far away from Denmark. However, Clausen's unrealistic and hazardous missionary plan eventually did not lead him to "the heathen" but to a brief visit to Norway. There he stayed with

Haugians in Bergen for a couple of weeks during Easter in 1841, preaching in their assemblies.

This experience was such a success for both parties that Clausen was immediately invited to come back for a longer trip around the mountainous country. First, however, Clausen visited Grundtvig in Copenhagen, fully acquiring his teaching about the Covenant of Baptism. Meeting Grundtvig was like a new awakening for Clausen, who now had a double motivation to go to Norway: both to be among the Haugians again and to convey to them Grundtvig's teachings about baptism. These were the real reasons for his five-month-long travel among Haugians in Norway in the summer of 1841. Clausen's travel to Norway was, in other words, a mission trip with a Grundtvigian message and had nothing to do with Clausen's poor health.[28] Considering his later rejection of Grundtvig's views, this was understandably something Clausen was not eager to stress in his autobiography.

The Need for Ordination

Fourth, why did Clausen eventually choose America over Africa? His whole life he had been planning to be a missionary, and through acquaintances in Norway he was finally given the chance. When he was offered to be the companion of Hans Schreuder on his upcoming mission to South Africa, in the end Clausen turned down the offer. In his autobiography he reasoned that "as long as he was not ordained, it would be practically impossible for him to accomplish anything" if Schreuder were to die abroad.[29]

Once again, it is impossible to understand Clausen's reasoning without Grundtvig. As explained above, Grundtvig's teaching was that God's saving grace was transmitted through baptism. Consequently, there was little point in being a missionary without being ordained, as there would be a need to baptize the heathen in order to bring them God's grace. In other words, Clausen would need to be ordained if he was going to be a missionary at all. An evident problem was that, years ago, Clausen deliberately had chosen not to study theology. He had, in other words, by his own choosing closed the door to ordination, and now it was too late to do anything about it. Neither in Norway nor in Denmark would the state church grant him ordination without proper qualification.[30] There was, however, a way out of the problem, but it involved traveling to a different place.

Figure 3. Plaque in Clausen City Park in the town of Saint Ansgar, Iowa. Photograph by Jostein Garcia de Presno.

According to Lutheran doctrine, ordination could be granted exceptionally if there was a group of Christians who called Clausen for pastoral service and if there were no other qualified pastors in the vicinity who could serve them. In South Africa, this would never be the case, as there were no Christians there from before. In America, however, there were already scores of Norwegian Christian immigrants who explicitly desired a pastor to serve them.[31] There were also German Lutheran immigrant pastors nearby who could perform such an exceptional ordination in the appropriate way.[32] This then considerably contributed to tipping the scale in favor of immigrating to the United States instead of becoming a missionary to Africa. From Clausen's autobiography, one might get the idea that the initiative for Clausen's ordination in Muskego came from the Norwegian settlers. The case was rather that this was part of Clausen's plan before immigrating and was an important motivation for doing so.[33]

The Other Reason: Martha

Finally, one other factor was decisive for Clausen in deciding to emigrate, and this was Martha Rasmussen. Clausen had become engaged to Martha soon after moving to Langeland and had no intentions of breaking off the engagement. In

Clausen's autobiography, Martha does not feature in the narrative of his decision to emigrate. From the letter to Hass and other letters from the same time, however, it is clear that she played a decisive part.[34] When Clausen returned to Denmark from his travel among Haugians in Norway, he was for a time considering enrolling as a student at a missionary institute that the Haugians were planning to set up in Stavanger the following year. Martha then made it clear that she did not see herself as a future missionary wife in Africa, and she therefore proposed to call off the engagement. Clausen refused, and the matter was left hanging.

When Clausen later was asked to join Schreuder in going to South Africa, he considered it only on condition that Martha approve. When he journeyed to Norway in 1842 for discussions with Schreuder and others, the subject was not only the possibility of ordination but also how to accommodate for Martha, who, according to Clausen, now had changed her mind about accompanying him. Not very surprisingly, it would be much more convenient for Martha to join Clausen in going to America than to Africa. When this surfaced as a possibility during Clausen's stay, it immediately seemed to present a better option.

When Clausen returned home again to Denmark in the fall of 1842, he had finally decided not to join Schreuder. Martha was overjoyed at his decision, having feared that he would leave her behind. He then proposed for her to join him in going to America instead, to which she readily agreed. The final consolidation of their commitment took place a few months later, when they got married on Langeland. Now there was no turning back. In April the following year, they left Denmark for good. It was probably paramount for Clausen's own self-perception that his emigration be seen as a fulfillment of his widely known call to mission. Perhaps it did not seem proper for a person who nurtured a desire to become a missionary to decide the question about service to God largely based on an engagement. Whatever the reason, Martha's role for Clausen's decision to emigrate was left out of his autobiography.

These five issues, then, once so prominent in the life and self-presentation of the young Clausen, were probably seen as inconvenient backstage secrets from the perspective of the retired Clausen in Minnesota. In the autobiography he composed there, they were given minor roles (the urge to be ordained, Martha) or left out altogether (family conflicts, anticlericalism, Grundtvigian mission). Clausen's two autobiographical accounts are not only years apart but also provide narratives that in some respects are worlds apart.

The Apology

Clausen's letter to Hass, which follows, was written after Clausen had returned from his visit to Schreuder in 1842. This time he had made a journey around another part of the country, preaching in Haugian assemblies, and was now about to set sail for Denmark. A few weeks earlier, he had announced his final decision not to join Schreuder in going to South Africa, and this news had reached his friend Hass in Denmark. Ludvig Hass (1808–1881) was himself about to set off as a missionary to Izmir (Smyrna), Turkey, and was extremely disappointed in Clausen.[35] He denounced him for all his changes of mind: for breaking off his legal studies, for aborting his theological studies, for leaving his revival activity in Denmark, and now for casting aside his call to be a missionary. Clausen's reply to Hass, printed below, was therefore an apology in the classical sense of the word: a defense. It was an attempt to explain the reasons behind all the changes of plan and to justify himself by showing that they all made sense if one just knew the whole story.

Clausen was, of course, at this time already strongly contemplating immigration to the United States. Interestingly, however, Clausen does not even mention this in his letter to Hass, even though he probably had already discussed this with Martha after his return and might even have made his decision. This could be due to concern that his plan would not materialize, yet again, as had been the case so many times before. This time, however, it did. One might only guess what Hass thought when he, a few months later, would learn about Clausen's immigration.

Letter from C. L. Clausen to L. D. Hass

Rifbjerg via Rudkjøbing,[36] September 10th, 1842[37]

My dearly beloved friend and brother in Christ! Mr. pastor L. D. Hass.

Now that I have returned home and found a bit of peace, it weighs heavily on my heart to write to you a few lines in response to your truly dear letter of the 3rd of last month, which I received in Christiansand after I had already come as far on the way home from Trondheim.[38] If my letter is to reach you in Copenhagen, then I must hurry as your stay there is likely not much longer. . . .

There is something I will tell you as a small appendix to what you have already heard of my life story, and which perhaps no one else could tell you, at least not better than I. And yet it seems to me that it is also necessary for you to know, as it may shed light on much that has been dark and incomprehensible to you so far. For while others, even my closest ones, could only have the opportunity to know and judge the instability in my outward decisions, they knew no more about my inner motives, or what was going on and stirring in my heart, than what I told them myself. And this was only little, especially in the beginning after my awakening, as I let others know about it, partly because it was still somewhat unclear to myself, and partly because at that time I feared my parents' anger and opposition if they truly came to know what my soul longed for day and night, namely, to be able to bring the great and precious Gospel to those who still sit in darkness and in the shadow of death.

As you may have heard, I was at an estate management office on Fyn when I was awakened from my state of sin to a new life in Christ. It was hard for me to be there after I could no longer find peace in sin. But I resisted as best I could, both within myself and around me, as ridicule and mockery of the grossest kind were part of the daily order. At times I longed for deliverance from this sodomitic life, I won't deny that, but I never dared entertain the thought or let any word escape my lips about leaving, until the three years I was supposed to be there (I still had half of the time left) were over in order to go to Copenhagen and continue my legal studies. Although even then the longing to go to the heathen had begun to awaken, it did not have much power or influence over me at that time.

Only when my father, in addition to the grocery outlet, acquired the farm where he now lives,[39] which happened at that time, and expressed a desire for me to come home, only then did I dare to allow that wish to take hold: to leave that ungodly manor and return to my dear family where I thought I would find desire and receptivity for God's word and the new life that flowed through me, and in their company to grow as a flourishing plant in the grace and knowledge of our Lord and Savior Jesus Christ.

That I thus left my legal career, no one who understands the circumstances rightly can attribute to me as fickleness. Neither had the steward with whom I was staying heard any complaint about me that could prompt my father to call me away. On the contrary, when my father requested of him that I should come home, he not only expressed his full satisfaction with me but also declared that he considered it wrong to divert me from the path I had started on. This he believed I was particularly suited for, especially since I had developed a desire for God's word, as it had contributed to making me even more calm and diligent.

However, when I came home, I found it to be quite different from what I had imagined. For my entire family was initially strongly opposed to me, as soon as they noticed that Christianity was not considered by me as mere empty talk, but that I wanted it to show its power in our lives and interactions as well. Nonetheless, things were bearable at first, until there was some serious awakening in various places in the parish.[40] This greatly angered the old pastor, Lauritz Ottesen, who was still alive at the time. Since he was afraid to involve himself directly in this matter by publicly opposing the gatherings, given that his conduct was so openly scandalous in several respects that he might well fear for his reputation,[41] he turned to my father, requesting that he strictly forbid me from conducting religious assemblies.

My eldest sister, who had up until then been strongly against me, had just been awakened at that time.[42] And if I had been zealous to punish sin and exhort to repentance, she became even more so. As a result, my father, who at that time still knew nothing of the life hidden with Christ in God,[43] naturally soon became angry, perhaps also due to our often and sternly repeated reminders and exhortations. Therefore, he immediately followed the pastor's urging to forbid me from conducting assemblies. And since I could not, and still do not believe I should, silence the testimony that stood vividly before my soul at that time, and which I clearly saw had worked and was working for the blessing of many souls previously secure in sin, the result was that I was expelled from my parents' house under curses and ridicule.

Oh, my beloved brother! Still, my eyes must bleed and my heart be deeply and sorrowfully bent and moved by vividly recalling those scenes. I have rarely touched upon this period in my life with anyone. And surely I would not with you either, if I did not owe you an explanation due to your sympathy and openness, which unfortunately brings me too much into contact with these heartbreaking and most humiliating events.

Since I came home, I had never thought of being anything other than a farmer. Sometimes, however, by thinking of the sad condition of the heathen, I felt an inexplicably strong impulse and longing permeate my soul to go to them and proclaim to them the glad tidings that salvation and blessedness are also to be obtained by them in Christ through mere grace without merit. At that time, it was far from me to conceive any actual thought, let alone determination, that I could or would come to accomplish this deed, which I regarded in my heart as the greatest and most glorious on earth. I was also of the conviction that we would soon be obliged to adopt a new liturgy and service book in the Danish state church, according to Bishop Mynster's proposal.[44] I, along with many others, would then expectedly leave the state church; and as for me, the country, at the same time. I imagined traveling to North America or a similar place where there is free exercise of religion, and still many thousands of heathen among the natives. There I could perhaps work as a missionary.[45]

Thus were my thoughts roughly before I was driven out of my parents' house for the first time. But these truly unexpected circumstances brought about, as you can imagine, a rather significant revolution in my entire way of thinking. However, you have probably never experienced such, and how should I then expect that you could truly understand my position? I regarded everything around me as utterly foreign. I considered my current pursuit to be ended in my native land. In my mind I was already shaking the dust off my feet to seek a new home and begin a new career among the heathen.

However, the shame of having driven me away solely for the sake of God's word, and, as I also believe, paternal love, soon moved my father to call me back again before I had even left Ærø. Only God knows how it would otherwise have gone with me at that time. I returned to my parents, with their permission to conduct assemblies freely, which I did. But now, the longing to go to the heathen had become almost irresistibly strong within me. The heathen and their misery were constantly on my mind during the day and in my dreams at night. The voice within me grew louder and stronger, convincing me that it was surely God's will for me to go to them, to proclaim to them his counsel and will for their salvation as a humble instrument in his hand. However, how and when I should achieve that remained and continued to be a mystery to me.

The revival on Ærø, however, continued to spread to different places, and with it the anger of the unbelievers. To my unspeakable joy, also my dear mother was awakened by God's grace to a true and serious life in Christ. But the more I rejoiced, the more my father was embittered. Further, since he probably believed that I was the cause of her awakening, as well as that of others, and thought that what he then called an evil could best be restrained by my removal, he commanded me to leave home again.

I traveled to Fyn, and since Peter Larsen Skræppenborg just then needed someone to teach his son and help out with his farming, he immediately hired me.[46] I stayed with him for about half a year.[47] Then my father fell ill. What moved him to call me back again, I can only guess at. But it is certain that he did, and I obeyed without objection, though certainly not without much inner struggle and many misgivings. That I should go to the heathen almost always stood firm in my mind. Indeed, I must openly admit that many times in recent times, I have not felt nearly as clearly, firmly, and steadily a calling, nor as alive and burning a longing for it, in my heart as I felt back then. But how was it to be realized? I asked myself this question thousands of times without ever getting a satisfactory answer. I prayed and I pondered, but the fog would not lift, and no way out appeared that I dared to follow with confidence.

Then my father hit upon the idea that I should become a pastor. In this he was encouraged by many who knew me, and countless suggestions were made to me in that regard. But becoming a pastor in the state church was always a great aversion to me for reasons that were almost inexplicable even to myself.[48] So why should I then proceed to study? Who could guarantee that my spiritual life would not be lost if I went to the ungodly university and my occupation mostly consisted of philosophical ponderings? This and many other concerns pressed upon my mind. I was already about to oppose the entire idea of studying when suddenly, like a lightning bolt, the thought arose within me: Yes, you can study to become a pastor; and when you have finished your exams, you can be sent out by the Church of Denmark as a missionary among the heathen. I didn't dwell on this for long before I had made up my mind and agreed that I would study theology.

The old pastor in Bregninge had died, and Provost Christensen had taken his place.[49] He immediately volunteered to help me prepare for my studies in the ancient languages, etc., and my daily schooling with him began right away. I grasped fairly well what I was supposed to learn, and the provost consistently gave much hope for my progress. But there was always a stumbling block for me that I couldn't overcome. I had indeed agreed to study theology, but I had not let anyone know the true intention behind it. It was clear to me that if my father knew that I was not to become a pastor in the Church of Denmark, but to travel as a missionary to the heathen, he would not spend a single penny on my studies. On the other hand, to let him hope that I would become a pastor in the Church of Denmark, and thus let him perhaps with difficulty finance my studies only to disappoint him completely in the end, I could not in good conscience do. But to tell him outright what the intention was, I had neither the courage nor the strength. This has often seemed strange to me afterward.

For a while, I struggled greatly with this matter internally. I prayed to the Lord for guidance, but I couldn't see any other option than to break off my studies. Hence, that is what I did. But I only gave the reason that I feared losing my spiritual life during my studies and that I believed I couldn't as a Christian become a pastor in the Church of Denmark, especially if, as we might expect, the new liturgy and service book were introduced. Perhaps I should have stated the real reason outright, but it never occurred to me at the time that it could be possible.

I was now through with studying, but by no means was I through with the mission cause. On the contrary, it had become a matter most close to my heart and soul. That I was fickle and unstable was the judgment I often heard. Though it saddened me to hear, I did not become angry. For in my heart, I knew I was free from these accusations regarding the matter itself. However, I also knew that to others who were not privy to my innermost thoughts, it could not appear otherwise. Thoughts conflicted within me, and perhaps I was too restless in my eagerness to see the desires of my soul fulfilled and like a child surrender myself in silence and patience under God's guidance and providence. At least, I often reproach myself with this.

I pondered on finding means and ways through which I could reach the heathen. I always felt that I needed some preparation and education for that purpose more than what I already had, but the thought never crossed my mind back then that I needed the church's consecration and ordination. I must admit that the inner calling in me was deep and strong, but my missionary ideas and plans were rather superficial and, I might add, somewhat idealistic. The essence of my longings and plans was to go to the heathen and awaken them with a living testimony. However, I never really thought about establishing and gathering congregations through baptism and communion in the proper ecclesiastical and apostolic order.[50] You can easily see, therefore, that for me the main goal was simply to get there and cry out for awakening and conversion among them.

Then a plan arose within me, which I not only must call fanatical but downright ungodly. However, I never imagined there could be the slightest evil in it. It was to go to sea, under the pretext of wanting to support myself in the future. But then, when I had gone far away to the heathen lands or at least near them, to desert the ship, and to travel among them and begin to work according to my plans. I am almost ashamed, dear brother, to write this, that in my fanaticism I could so completely forget the holy bonds and duties that tied me to family, friends, and homeland. But I would be a thousand times more ashamed if now, while I clearly see and condemn that fanaticism and ungodliness, I were to be guilty of something much worse, namely, to break a sacred promise,[51] which I myself, with deliberate mind and in prayer to the Lord, have made, and to tear apart a bond whereby perhaps hearts would be irreparably wounded and, moreover, such ungodliness would be imputed to the Lord and his work! I am sure you understand, dear brother! I will explain myself better later.

With that plan firmly in mind, I then applied to the king to be granted a permission for marine travel, without which I could not be hired on any ship.[52] I now prepared myself every day to leave as soon as I could get the approval and a job. But things turned out quite differently from what I had imagined. A hasty action by my father toward one of the servants, in which he drove him away without him actually having deserved it, aroused my zeal. I openly criticized his actions and urged him, as best I could, to make amends for the offense. This only had the effect of him driving me as well away in his anger and forbidding me from ever crossing his threshold again. This was the third time I had to leave my parents' house like this, and I was certainly not in the best mood as I packed my few belongings and set off on the journey.

A rather tense relationship had long prevailed between me and my father, but by keeping silent and complying with him as much as possible in recent times, we had avoided a public rupture. But now that it had happened, a considerable anger and defiance filled my mind. I considered my cause to be the most just in the world. Even this occurrence I immediately declared as a sign and guidance from the Lord that it was definitely his will for me to travel in the aforementioned manner, and the sooner the better. For I now had nothing to wait for. Alas, how deceitful is the human heart in its devices and hidden motives, who can ever fathom it?

Driven out of my parents' house, I wandered aimlessly for a while. I had almost decided to spend the time in this way until I could leave. However, I came to Langeland during this wandering and held religious assemblies in various places, including here in Simmerbølle parish.[53] And since the widow[54] here in Rifbjerg and Rasmus Madsen,[55] who was then in Kassebølle (but now is in Zealand), had, with the permission of the Chancellery, taken their children out of school and now needed someone to teach them, I took on this task at their request.[56]

I had not intended to stay here longer than the winter, at most, and in the following spring seek employment and leave. But when I became acquainted with Martha Rasmussen,[57] and increasingly developed love for her and also won her reciprocal love, that plan of mine became more and more repugnant to think of carrying out. Our mutual love, Martha's and mine, could not remain hidden from us for long. I had some reservations about entering into a closer and binding relationship with her, and I had many struggles during prayer to the Lord about what I should do. Whether or not I received certainty, the result was this: We confessed our love to each other and, that if it was God's will and He did not place any significant obstacle in our path, we would enter into matrimony with each other.

Meanwhile, I received approval for my application to the king and was granted the permission for marine travel. But the plan for which I intended to use it had meanwhile become out-of-date. The bond that was formed between Martha and me through our engagement was new and strong, and I felt that if it were to break, it would be akin to my heart breaking. Yet, it had to be over between us if I were to carry out the permission. Moreover, upon closer consideration of the plan itself, I soon realized its poor, fanatical, and blatantly ungodly nature, so I immediately rejected it with the greatest shame and disgust. However, since I now had the approval and was registered in the maritime register, I decided, partly to avoid being seen as a fool who would not use the approval I had worked so hard to obtain, and partly to stay on the maritime register and thus be exempted from military service, to go on some sea voyages and then later quietly pursue some livelihood in the countryside.

But already on the first sea voyage to Bergen, I had several recurrent apoplectic episodes, which forced me to stay home after the first journey.[58]

However, I was constantly in a strange mood regarding the mission cause, for I still felt the same longing in my heart to go to the heathen. But now I dared not entertain the idea or give it any room. Immediately after my return from Bergen was the first time I visited and conversed with Grundtvig and Lindberg.[59] God granted me grace to receive enlightenment through these two chosen instruments in many matters that had been dark and confused to me before concerning the holy universal church, its foundation and propagation, its pillars and means of grace.

I immediately gained entirely different concepts than I had previously held about mission work among the heathen. I must sincerely thank God that he had allowed obstacles to arise in my path so that my previous plans had not been carried out. Although I still felt the same drive and calling in my heart for this work as before, it had now become a matter of conscience for me that if I were to carry out missionary work among the heathen, I must also be authorized and equipped for it by the church, by way of ordination and consecration. As it was, I saw no way for me to obtain such an ordination, except through some almost impossible means, so I endeavored as best I could to remain calm and let the Lord guide as He would.

At that time, I received various invitations from Norway to travel through the country to conduct religious assemblies, as there was such a great need for new revival, encouragement, and enlightenment. Since I felt a strong urge to work in such a way as was not as feasible and free here in this country, I undertook, with the approval of several friends, a journey through the southern part of Norway, as you know well.[60] This journey and activity, I hope, was not without benefit by God's grace, although it was only in great weakness.[61]

In Stavanger, there were already many people actively working toward establishing a missionary institute in Norway where those who felt the desire and calling could be trained to go out to the heathen as missionaries.[62] This reignited in me, with renewed vigor, the longing that had been slumbering for some time. Here, I could be prepared, ordained, and properly sent out, and as I hoped, also bring along my beloved Martha, if she was willing and if it would otherwise be God's will. I discussed the matter itself with the mission enthusiasts, and they declared unanimously that they wished me to come there if the institute was established. However, I didn't mention anything about Martha until I had spoken with her about it myself. When I returned home, I spoke with her about it, but she didn't feel she could do it. She thought it would be best if I went alone and our engagement end. But I couldn't do that, and so it remained as it was between us.

To recount here every single event of the past year regarding this matter would be far too lengthy and also pointless, as you are likely quite familiar with it. I must only note that Martha changed her decision and would gladly accompany me if I were to travel away. And when I last went to Norway to investigate whether it could be done, or if it was God's will for me to accompany candidate Schreuder,[63] it was by no means with the thought that she would stay behind if I went but rather that I could not or would not go with the candidate unless she could also come along. Though, I believe she would have been content to remain at home if I had wanted it that way and would have considered it to be God's will.

However, while at home I didn't have much hope or expectation about being able to accompany Schreuder. For I soon saw many difficulties that would get in the way. I essentially went this time,[64] as before, to travel around and talk to people about their salvation. In general, I got along well with Schreuder regarding his missionary plans and found in him a very fine and Christian man, whom I would have been very inclined to follow if it were indeed God's will. However, the difficulties of obtaining ecclesiastical ordination immediately presented themselves, as I had expected.

Upon the advice of several people, I wrote to Lindberg to obtain information about whether I, as an unstudied person, could expect to be ordained in Denmark. That I expressed my decision to follow Schreuder in this letter, as definitively as you suggest, I cannot recall, and I hardly believe it to be the case.[65] In any event, it was certainly not so and must either be due to unclear wording on my part or a misunderstanding upon your reading the letter. For while I did indeed wish to follow him (and once all obstacles were cleared, I hoped it could happen), it was evident that this was not to be, since I could not expect to be ordained in Norway, and it was highly doubtful to me whether it could happen in Denmark. However, it is certain that even if I could have been ordained immediately either in Norway or Denmark, I would not have pursued it unless I had first obtained permission to bring Martha, which I do not think would have posed any obstacle. On my journey from Christiania to Trondheim, however, I became ill and weak the whole time, so much so that, after receiving Lindberg's response to my letter—which also did not give me much hope—I could not consider this matter for the time being.

Now I intend to stay quietly at home for the first part of the winter, especially since I am still considerably weak, although somewhat better than I have been. I am considering whether it is God's will for me to enter into marriage with my dear Martha this autumn, in the hope that many struggles will cease, which now sometimes cause heartache. However, there will surely always be enough and more than I can imagine. I do not know how God will lead me in the future, but strangely enough, despite all obstacles and resistance, the same longing and the same hope continue to stand unwaveringly in my soul: that I will one day proclaim God's word to the heathen. I cannot, with all my strength, erase this longing and hope from my heart, nor do I dare to try. . . .

What I have written here in the foregoing are truths, most of which have never been told by me to anyone before, as I couldn't or can't believe that anyone else has experienced such things. Yet, I felt strongly compelled to tell you, partly because I didn't want you to depart with such poor thoughts about me, which you likely must have had to some extent based on rumors, and partly because I expect that your advice and experiences will enlighten me by God's grace. May the Lord, before whose face and in whose name I have written this, accompany it with His grace, that it may be for His glory and our mutual benefit. . . .

Be now greeted a thousand times from me and my dear Martha. We wish all of God's grace and blessings for your heart and your work. . . . Your very devoted and affectionate friend and brother in Christ!

Claus Lauritzen Clausen

PS. I do not wish this letter to be read by any stranger. However, if you would like to show it to Lindberg, I have no objection.

__Jostein Garcia de Presno__ is associate professor of the history of Christianity at Volda University College. He has studied the development of the nineteenth-century Norwegian Haugian movement and is currently working on a book about Claus L. Clausen and his involvement with Norwegian Haugians.

NOTES

The article is based on Jostein Garcia de Presno, *I Hans Nielsen Hauges fotspor. Claus L. Clausens dagbøker fra en reise til Norge i 1841* (forthcoming).

1. See, for example, Hjalmar Rued Holand, *Norwegians in America: The Last Migration* (1930; Center for Western Studies, Augustana College, 1978), 113–25; E. Clifford Nelson and Eugene L. Fevold, *The Lutheran Church Among Norwegian-Americans* (Augsburg Publishing House, 1960), 82–95; Odd Sverre Lovoll, *The Promise of America: A History of the Norwegian-American People,* rev. ed. (University of Minnesota Press, published in cooperation with the Norwegian American Historical Association, 1999), 80–82, 104. Clausen has also been the subject of several biographical accounts, the most important of which are Svein Strand, "Pastor C. L. Clausen," *Symra: Et skrift for norske paa begge sider av havet* 9 (1913): 204–23; Rasmus Andersen, *Pastor Claus Laurits Clausen* (Danish Lutheran Publishing House, 1921); A. Margareth Jorgensen, "Claus L. Clausen: Pioneer Pastor and Settlement Promoter, 1843–1868" (master's thesis, University of Minnesota, 1930); H. Fred Swansen, *The Founder of St. Ansgar: The Life Story of Claus Laurits Clausen* (Lutheran Publishing House, 1949). The most recent account of Clausen's career is Thomas E. Jacobson, "The Varied Career of Claus Lauritz Clausen," presented at the Lutheran Historical Conference Biennial Meeting, Concordia Seminary, October 2022.
2. *Folkebladet,* 14 August 1907, my translation.
3. Clausen's autobiography is cited at length in Andersen, *Pastor Claus Laurits Clausen,* 11–15. All quotations in this section are my translations of the Danish original. Rather interestingly, Clausen formulated his autobiography in the third person, as if intending for it to be published exactly the way he wrote it.
4. Andersen, 13.

5. Andersen, 13.
6. Andersen, 14.
7. Andersen, 15.
8. The most comprehensive account of the debate is given in Brynjar Haraldsø, "Slaveridebatten i Den norske synode: En undersøkelse av slaveridebatten i Den norske synode i USA i 1860-årene med særlig vekt på debattens kirkelig-teologiske aspekter" (Solum, 1988).
9. For an introduction to the Danish theologian, historian, poet, and politician, see A. M. Allchin, *N. F. S. Grundtvig: An Introduction to His Life and Work* (Aarhus University Press, 1997).
10. A brief but excellent English résumé of Grundtvig's so-called matchless discovery of 1825 is given in Kaj Baagø, "Grundtvigs mageløse opdagelse. Et bidrag til dens tilblivelses-historie," *Grundtvig-Studier* 10, no. 1 (1957): https://doi.org/10.7146/grs.v10i1.13229.
11. "Synodalforhandlinger," *Kirkelig Maanedstidende* 6, no. 8 (1861): 234.
12. See E. C. Nelson and E. L. Fevold, *The Lutheran Church Among Norwegian-Americans,* vol. 1 (Augsburg Publishing House, 1960).
13. Such was, for instance, the case when the Clausens moved from Muskego to Luther Valley in 1846. See "Menighedens Grundlæggelse og dens Forhandlinger" [Account of the foundation and negotiations of the congregation], in the Luther Valley Church Records, p. 448.
14. *Evangelisk Luthersk Kirketidende,* 24 November 1876.
15. See, for instance, H. A. Preus et al., *Om Pastor C. L. Clausens "Gjenmæle"* (Decorah, Iowa: B. Anundsen, 1870), 2.
16. Søren Bache, *Et minneskrift fra Gamle Muskego 1839–1847* (Per A. Holst Forlag, 2010), 62, 83, 90, 99.
17. In Danish historiography, the revival goes under the name of the "godly assembly-movement."
18. The Conventicle Act, or the decree of 13 January 1741, was the same for Denmark and Norway. It prohibited religious assemblies (larger than a gathering of household members) without the presence of the local pastor.
19. Pedersen, "Den gudelige Forsamlingsbevægelse," in *De fynske Vækkelser,* ed. Anders Pontoppdan Thyssen, Vækkelsernes Frembrud i Danmak i første Halvdel af det 10. Århundrede (GEC Gads Forlag, 1964), 313.
20. Clausen never saw his parents again after immigrating. When he visited his fatherland in 1867, they had already passed away.
21. An interesting fact is that the children that Clausen tutored belonged to revivalists. These children were homeschooled so as not to be negatively influenced by the alleged lack of true Christian teachings at the public school.
22. The translation is my own. The original Danish hymn has fourteen verses and is cited in its entirety in Andersen, *Pastor Claus Laurits Clausen,* 17–20.
23. Eielsen founded the Evangelical Lutheran Church in America in 1846, more commonly known as the Eielsen Synod. He was an outspoken critic of the Norwegian Synod with its strong ties to the Church of Norway.
24. Quotation from the letter to Hass in this article.

25. The protagonist in the Baptist mission to Denmark was a former Jew, Julius Købner, who described his experiences in Julius Købner, *Revival of Religion in Denmark: Including an Account of the Rise and Present State of the Baptist Churches in That Kingdom* (London: Houlston and Stoneman, Ward and Co., 1841).
26. Pedersen, "Den gudelige Forsamlingsbevægelse," 315.
27. The Haugians got their name from the Norwegian revivalist Hans Nielsen Hauge (1771–1824). A good English introduction to Hauge and the Haugian revival is given in Alison Heather Stibbe, "Hans Nielsen Hauge and the Prophetic Imagination" (PhD diss., University of London, 2007), 20–25.
28. Clausen certainly had health issues already as a young man, but his travels to Norway had nothing to do with this. Upon returning to Denmark, Clausen clearly described his views on baptism in an article for the journal *Dannebroge.* See Clausen to J. C. Lindberg, undated, Lindberg's archive, 369:3 Gendøberne, Royal Library of Copenhagen.
29. About Schreuder's role in early Norwegian missions, see John Nome, *Demringstid i Norge: Fra misjonsinteresse til misjonsselskap* (Det norske misjonsselskap, 1942), 352–69.
30. Grundtvig's companion in Copenhagen, Jacob C. Lindberg (1797–1857), counseled Clausen in a number of matters before Clausen's immigration. Lindberg maintained that there might be a chance for Clausen to obtain ordination in Denmark but warned that it would require extensive studying.
31. About seventy settlers in Muskego signed the petition for Clausen's ordination in 1843.
32. The pastor who ordained Clausen was Reverend L. F. Krause in Milwaukee. Eva Jean Rethwisch, *The History of Luther Valley Lutheran Church* (Luther Valley Lutheran Church, 2000), 22–24.
33. The letter of calling from the congregation was even drafted by Clausen himself, according to Bache, *Et minneskrift,* 59.
34. In a letter to Lindberg dated 22 March 1843, Clausen describes in detail how his engagement to Martha was crucial for his final decision. Clausen to J. C. Lindberg, 22 March 1843, Lindberg's archive, 922 4° Letters to Lindberg, Royal Library of Copenhagen.
35. Ludvig Koch, "Hass, Ludvig Daniel," in *Dansk biografisk Lexikon,* ed. C. F. Bricka (Kjøbenhavn: Gyldendalske Boghandels Forlag, 1887–1905).
36. Rifbjerg was Martha's hometown and the town Clausen himself resided in on Langeland.
37. The Danish original is Clausen to L. D. Hass, 10 September 1842, Lindberg's Archive, 922 4° box XIII, Letters to and from Others than J. C. Lindberg, Royal Library of Copenhagen (my translation). Parts of the letter containing greetings and other matter of little bearing on Clausen's biography have been left out, as indicated by ellipses [. . .].
38. On this second journey around Norway, Clausen traveled north from Oslo to Trondheim and then south along the coast to Kristiansand. From there he returned by ship to Langeland.
39. Clausen's father had a farm grocery and traded in horses. At this time, he also acquired a farm on Ærø and needed Clausen's help running it.
40. The revival on Ærø started in 1837.
41. Lauritz Ottesen, the pastor of Bregninge parish on Ærø, was known to have a problem with alcohol.
42. This was Anne Maria Clausen.

43. The formulation indicates that Clausen's father also eventually joined the revival.
44. Bishop Jacob P. Mynster of Copenhagen proposed a new liturgy and liturgical book for the Church of Denmark in 1838. After much public debate and opposition from the revivalists, it was dropped, never to be implemented.
45. Already this early, Clausen was contemplating going to North America. At this time, however, he saw himself as working as a missionary among "the heathen," not as a pastor.
46. Peter Larsen Skræppenborg (1802–1873) was a prominent Danish revivalist preacher from Fyn.
47. Church records indicate that Clausen's stay on Fyn probably lasted only two to three months.
48. Denmark (like Norway and Sweden) was a confessional Evangelical-Lutheran monarchy at the time, and the king was the head of the church.
49. In 1835, H. C. Christensen was the provost in Ærø and succeeded Ottesen in Bregninge after Ottesen passed away in 1839.
50. Clausen here echoes important elements of Grundtvig's theology.
51. Clausen is referring to his engagement with Martha Rasmussen, see below.
52. *Permission for marine travel*: Literally "temporary sea permission." A personal permission, granted by the king, that transferred the applicant from the army to the navy, which was necessary for traveling by sea.
53. In 1838, the revival started spreading to Langeland. In other words, Clausen was moving to the hot spot of the revival.
54. The widow of Christen Jensen was active in the revival on Langeland. For a time, her house was the center of the revival on the island.
55. Rasmus Madsen was one of the leaders of the revival on Langeland. He later sided with the Baptists.
56. Clausen was hired as a private tutor to a handful of revivalist children. The parents did not want their children exposed to the public school teacher, whom they accused of being a "soul-murderer" since he denied the existence of hell. See Anders Pontoppdan Thyssen, "Den langelandske Vækkelse," in *De fynske Vækkelser,* ed. Anders Pontoppdan Thyssen, Vækkelsernes Frembrud i Danmak i første Halvdel af det 10. Århundrede (GEC Gads Forlag, 1964), 350–55.
57. Martha Fredrikke Rasmussen (1815–1846) was from Rifbjerg on Langeland.
58. Already in his young years, Clausen had seizures of different kinds.
59. About Grundtvig, see Allchin, *N. F. S. Grundtvig*; about Lindberg, see note 30.
60. Clausen traveled to Drammen and on to Christiania, Kongsberg, Numedal, Bergen, Svanøy, Stavanger, Kristiansand, and Arendal. During his journey, he kept a diary. See Jostein Garcia de Presno, *I Hans Nielsen Hauges fotspor. Claus L. Clausens dagbøker fra en reise til Norge i 1841* (forthcoming).
61. *In great weakness*: A pietistic expression indicating that whatever good might have come from the journey, the glory was due to God, not personal merit.
62. Clausen sat in on a meeting with Haugians for the establishment of a missionary institute while on his travels. The plan was for the institute to be up and going already in 1842, so Clausen's original plan was to enroll there. However, due to lack of faculty, the institute was delayed until 1843. By then Clausen had already decided to emigrate to America.

63. Hans P. S. Schreuder became the first missionary of Det norske Misjonsselskap, which was founded in 1842. Clausen had met many of the founders on his travel in Norway the year before and discussed his desire to become a missionary with them.
64. *This time*: In 1842.
65. Clausen is here defending himself against criticism from Hass that he had changed his mind yet again, after originally having agreed to join Schreuder to Africa.

A Feminism of Its Own

REVISITING THE SCANDINAVIAN-AMERICAN *WOMAN AND HOME*, CIRCA 1888–1920

Mona Holm

Introduction

The Scandinavian-American magazine *Woman and Home* (*Kvinden og Hjemmet*) was established in 1888 in Cedar Rapids, Iowa, by Norwegian-American Ida Hansen, whose aim, as editor, was to give "Scandinavian-borne women . . . knowledge of what was required of those who settled and lived in America . . . [and] help them in their desires to become good citizens."[1] Her venture was a success. For decades the magazine had a circulation of between 60,000 and 83,000, far exceeding that of the largest Norwegian newspaper at that time, the Norwegian-American *Skandinaven*.[2] Clearly, Scandinavian-American women were eager for news of particular concern to themselves.

From the beginning, editor Hansen and her team had sought to inform their readers of women's progress in all parts of the world, especially with respect to woman suffrage and women's emancipation more generally. The

Figure 1. Ida Hansen, born Jensen, circa 1870–1875. Photograph by Rohde & Schultz, 90 West Ohio St., Cor. Milwaukee Avenue, Chicago. Courtesy of Bryan Timm.

journal's name, *Woman and Home,* presented a contrast to this goal, however. Rather than pointing outward to the public and societal roles of women in America and beyond, it signaled that the home was a woman's place. This raises several questions, such as how the editors of this Scandinavian-American magazine set their priorities and what feminism meant to them.

This article explores *Woman and Home* with an emphasis on the magazine's coverage of feminism and women's issues. Historian Jon Gjerde demonstrates that immigrant culture was a culture of its own; in the case of Norwegian Americans, it was a hybrid of Norwegian and American cultures, with migrants developing complementary identities.[3] This suggests that actors promoting liberal and progressive ideas within an immigrant culture were likely addressing a population accustomed to different worldviews. Were Scandinavian-American women familiar with different worldviews on feminism? And did *Woman and Home* represent a feminism already familiar to them or did it produce a feminism specific to its readers, and if so, in what way?

Woman and Home may be classified as an early feminist ladies' magazine. This is a term media historian Synnøve Skarsbø Lindtner gives to a special category of women's magazines in the 1970s and 1980s. These publications combined a feminist agenda with the typical commercial ladies' magazine concept, with great parts of their content addressed specifically to housewives. They looked like ladies' magazines, but they discussed and defined the feminist cause. In this way, they sought to build a bridge between the entertaining weekly press and the feminist movement's women's magazines, the purpose of which was to inform, create debate, and mobilize women in multiple ways.[4]

This article argues that *Woman and Home* played an important role as an advocate for woman suffrage and women's rights among Scandinavian immigrant women in North America. It did so by combining arguments from the immigrants' old and new home countries, not least by simultaneously promoting both traditional and modern values (at times, in seemingly improbable ways). Additionally, because *Woman and Home* depended on subscriptions for its revenue, its editorial staff sought to avoid a progressive feminist image so as not to scare off their subscribers. This business strategy worked. The magazine brought a feminist message to a large audience and created pro-suffragist sentiment in an unthreatening format that celebrated women as homemakers.

This finding raises questions about the claim that Norwegian Americans and Norwegians were exceptional among immigrant groups with respect to their embrace of progressive ideas or their self-image as progressive. Anna M. Peterson argues that this belief was successfully deployed by Norwegian-American feminists to convince people of Norwegian and Scandinavian descent to support woman suffrage in the United States. Pointing to the advances in women's rights that took place in Norway from 1901 onward, they argued that those of Norwegian and Scandinavian ethnicity should embrace this progressive tradition.[5]

My examination of *Woman and Home,* however, suggests that Scandinavian-American women were more like than different from other immigrant women with respect to their receptivity to progressive ideas. Donna Gabaccia demonstrates that immigrant women and men in the United States had to operate in different realms because of the strength of the American ideal of domesticity. Among white, native-born, middle-class Americans, married women were expected to dedicate themselves to the house and their children. They were not to have paid work outside the home.[6] This ideal, or norm, was decisive for immigrant women and for their acceptance by the Anglo-American society.[7] The very title of the Scandinavian-American women's magazine and its discrepancy with the journal's feminist editorial platform suggests that the editors sought acceptance within the context of American society. *Woman and Home* is thus a relevant source for anyone interested in the cultural mediation between Scandinavians and Anglo-Americans and other immigration groups around 1900, not just for students of feminism. In this article, however, I focus on cultural norms of womanhood and femininity and on feminist ideas and how they were mediated, negotiated, and translated between Scandinavian newcomers, first- and second-generation Scandinavian Americans, Anglo-Americans, and other American citizens and immigrants. I view *Woman and Home* as a contact zone, a place where norms and values meet and are negotiated.[8] Although the magazine specifically addressed Scandinavian women, with Norwegian immigrant women making up its largest group of readers, it interests me as a mediator between Norwegian-American women and American society.

The use here of the term *contact zone* is drawn from the work of historian Judith Becker on European missions. Becker identifies three dimensions of contact: the specific historical context in which the contact takes place; an imagined contact between actors living in different geographical locations, manifested in written source material; and personal contact, which is an individual's incorporation of different cultures. This third type of contact, which resembles Gjerde's concept of complementary identities, renders individuals as contact zones themselves—or cultural brokers—between different cultures. *Woman and Home* and its editorial staff may be thought of as cultural brokers along similar lines as the missionaries in Becker's study.[9]

This article analyzes the magazine *Woman and Home* and its notions of feminism to better understand the cultural negotiations between American society and Scandinavian-American women and between the ideal of domesticity and feminist activism and the role of public women's magazines in these negotiations. Empirically, it examines key issues of the magazine from its initial year, 1888, as well as from succeeding decades. In addition, it draws on other Scandinavian-American, Norwegian, and Anglo-American newspapers and magazines from the 1880s through the 1920s, as well as scholarly literature, including Åse Elin Langeland's pioneering work on *Woman and Home,* published in 2009. I begin with the ambitions of the editor, Ida Hansen, and how she established the magazine. I then analyze *Women and Home*'s business model and editorial platform and explore its notions of womanhood, femininity, and feminism and its concurrent strong focus on traditional gender values. Finally, I consider the way that the magazine represented Scandinavian-American women's complementary identity and whether they both developed a distinctive feminism—a "feminism of their own."

Dedicated to Scandinavian Immigrant Women

The Scandinavian- and Norwegian-language press flourished in the United States in the 1880s. Scandinavian immigrant writers, editors, and publishers had, since the first Scandinavian-American newspaper, *Skandinavia,* appeared in 1847, launched a series of publications targeting the rapidly growing numbers of Norwegian, Danish, and Swedish immigrants in the United States. In the years 1865 to 1890, as many as 346,477 people emigrated from Norway alone, and by 1900, almost 513,000 had left their country, mainly to go to North America.[10] Due to their very similar written languages, Norwegians, Swedes, and Danes represented a growing market for Scandinavian publications. Newspapers were the main source of information at the time, and the selection available in the United States was impressive. As one of the Norwegian-American press pioneers expressed it: America was "the Land of Newspapers."[11] The newspapers printed in Scandinavian languages were diverse, ranging from conservative to socialist, freethinking to dogmatic Lutheranism. Nevertheless, no publication dedicated to women existed prior to the appearance of *Woman and Home* in 1888.[12]

The magazine's founder and editor was Ida Hansen, born Jensen. Its formal title was *Woman and Home: A Monthly Journal for the Scandinavian Woman in America* (*Et Maanedskrift for den Skandinaviske Kvinde i Amerika*).[13] The publication appeared in May 1888 and ran until August 1947. Editor Hansen was herself an immigrant from Ringsaker in Norway. She was brought up in a socially engaged family that highly valued education.[14] She arrived in the United States as a seventeen-year-old, together with her parents and three siblings, in 1870. The family settled in Chicago, where Ida met her future husband and business partner, Niels Frederick Hansen, a Dane. The couple married in 1875 and eventually had seven children. In 1884, they settled in Cedar Rapids, Iowa, where Niels Frederick Hansen the same year founded the magazine *For All Countries* (*For alle Lande*).[15] Ida Hansen was the editor of its section "The Housewife" ("Husmoderen"). After four years, *For All Countries* was discontinued, and Ida decided to launch her own publication entirely dedicated to women.

Ida Hansen received help with the new magazine from her younger sister Mina Jensen, who had been trained in printing techniques and had been the printer for *For All Countries*. Ida Hansen also sought advice from a network of housewives, probably established when she was editing the column "The Housewife." Hansen's husband became the magazine's publisher and business manager.[16]

Ida Hansen wanted the magazine to become a medium for exchange of thoughts and knowledge among its readers. Maintaining a dialogue with subscribers and building a sense of belonging—among readers as well as magazine staff—to a special community or network became an important part of the business model. In the second issue of *Woman and Home,* dated June 1888, Ida Hansen sent her regards to everyone who, after reading the first issue, had written letters of support for the new magazine.[17] This became her standard way of communicating with the readership. In this way, *Woman and Home* established itself as a contact zone, providing a space for communication between newly arrived and more experienced immigrant women living in different geographic

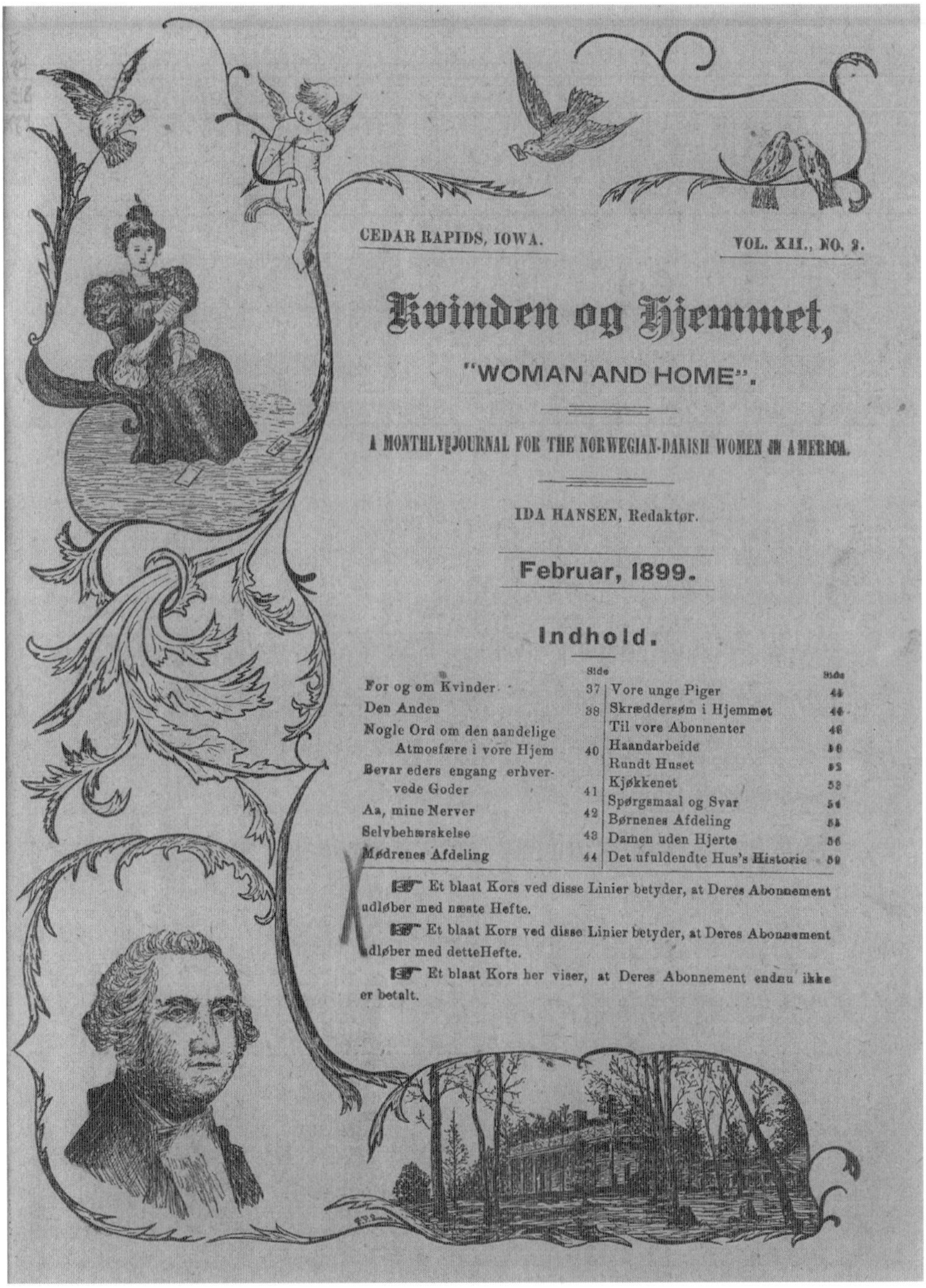

CEDAR RAPIDS, IOWA. VOL. XII., NO. 2.

Kvinden og Hjemmet,

"WOMAN AND HOME".

A MONTHLY JOURNAL FOR THE NORWEGIAN-DANISH WOMEN IN AMERICA.

IDA HANSEN, Redaktør.

Februar, 1899.

Indhold.

☞ Et blaat Kors ved disse Linier betyder, at Deres Abonnement udløber med næste Hefte.

☞ Et blaat Kors ved disse Linier betyder, at Deres Abonnement udløber med detteHefte.

☞ Et blaat Kors her viser, at Deres Abonnement endnu ikke er betalt.

Figure 2. Cover page of *Woman and Home*, February 1899, with table of contents, a romantic drawing, and an image of George Washington. Image courtesy of Vesterheim Norwegian-American Museum, Decorah, Iowa.

locations. Hansen showed her readers that they were important and that she was interested in their opinions. The magazine was not intended to be a one-way communication and had from the beginning several columns, including "Our Letterbox" ("Vor Brevkasse"), dedicated to the readers' own letters.

A Dear Monthly Guest "on a Rough Prairie, in a Deep Forest, or in a Big City"

Although subscribers to the magazine were scattered across the United States, as testified to by the return addresses on their letters to the editor, a large number, unsurprisingly, lived in the Midwestern states where most Norwegian and Scandinavian immigrants settled. Norwegians were the most agrarian of all the ethnic groups in the United States, and they sought farmland on the Great Plains. With the shift from family migration to individual migration in the 1880s, a gender difference emerged within the Norwegian immigrant population. Now, more unmarried young Norwegian women than men settled in urban areas and in the large cities such as Chicago, New York, Boston, Minneapolis, and Seattle, where they had more job opportunities. Most became domestic servants or maids.[18] These residential patterns are reflected in the letters to *Woman and Home*.

In a retrospective published in the 1930s, the magazine provided insight into its significance to its readers over the decades: "How often have we not . . . received letters from readers expressing something like: 'When *Woman and Home* arrives, it's like a party in the house. The magazine brings something like a breath of fresh air from my homeland.' "[19] The editors go on to explain how the magazine had helped its readers through difficult moments as immigrants trying to adjust to a new culture: "Anyone who has tried living in a lonely home, whether it was out on a rough prairie, in a deep forest, or in a big city, will attest to this. Being able to read something in the language of one's homeland—in the language of the heart—has certainly helped many a lonely immigrant through a difficult time of trial."[20] Although written by the editors, the text still testifies to the value of *Woman and Home* to many immigrants. It also indicates that the magazine was read in both rural and urban homes across the United States. In fact, it even had subscribers beyond the US borders, in Canada, Scandinavia, and Schleswig.[21] In the thousands of homes that received the magazine each

FIRST AVENUE, LOOKING EAST FROM FIRST STREET

Figure 3. The Hansen Publishing Company was, in its earlier years, run out of 414 First Avenue, Cedar Rapids. Photograph from Charles B. Armstrong, *Glimpses of Cedar Rapids* (Cedar Rapids, IA: Republican Printing Co., 1898). Courtesy of Linn County Historical Society.

month, it was often read by everyone in the family, even the men. According to Mrs. J. E. P. from Illinois, writing to the magazine in 1918, "husband and wife read *Woman and Home* with equal interest."[22]

A Promise to Keep Up with the Times

Ida Hansen explained her aims in publishing *Woman and Home* on the first page of the magazine's first issue, dated May 1888: "The magazine will become a medium for exchange of thoughts and opinions [for women], as well as experiences in the more practical work." Hansen then listed the topics the magazine would cover. In addition to "the woman's spiritual position" (*Kvindens aandelige Standpunkt*), she promised to provide information on "sewing and needlework, the nursery, flowers and the kitchen garden, . . . the kitchen, domestic advice, etc." She also presented her plans for a column named "Around the House," which would contain "tips regarding furnishing, arrangement and maintenance of the house." She added that the magazine might offer a section on chicken breeding as well, and if it turned out to be in line with the subscribers' wishes, a small story in each issue.[23]

While she promised material to expand the mind, Hansen also assured that there would be plenty of content to help immigrant women perform their daily work as housewives in their new country. Since most Norwegian immigrants lived in rural areas, *Woman and Home* expected many of its readers would be farm women. Yet in describing the content, Hansen made little mention of farm work. This was likely reflective of her adjustment mission. Women's work was defined differently in Scandinavia and in the United States. In Norway, women on farms worked outside in the fields during harvest. They cared for the cows and did the milking. In America, tending to the cattle and working in the fields were men's jobs. Anglo-American women were supposed to work inside the house, with the exceptions of tending the kitchen garden and raising chickens.[24] Hansen's magazine content would reflect this "new" division of labor.

Hansen further stated that *Woman and Home* would keep up with the times and give its readers "the best possible reading material" with the help of translations of material from "the best magazines" in other languages and articles from magazines "from home."[25] She added: "Otherwise, all contributions dealing with matters of interest to women, as well as articles on women's rights and anything that can serve to promote women's independence, will be gratefully received."[26] Hansen thus aimed to bring together information from both the old and the new homelands, to keep readers informed about news from abroad as well as about modern life in America. From the very beginning, she made clear that *Woman and Home* was to be a platform for feminist ideas.

Ida Hansen's introductory text showed her confidence in her project. However, having started something that no other Scandinavian-American woman had done, she suspected that some would view her project with skepticism: "Many will probably pull a smile when they receive this magazine and think: A magazine published and edited by women—no, that's not possible. Now, why not? As far as I know, we are indeed the first among the Scandinavians to have tried it; but in other nations it is not so uncommon."[27] She then explained the situation in the United States: "Here in America, there are several such magazines in the English language, which have not only managed to keep things going but have even been successful." Her final words to her readers on this matter: "Do we as a nation need to stand back for others? I mean, no!"[28]

Ida Hansen seems to have wanted to convince the Norwegian and Scandinavian Americans that their ethnic groups needed to keep up with the development in their new country. It is not clear whether Hansen was including all Scandinavians in the term *nation*.[29] Nevertheless, she did state that immigrants in some way still belong to their country of origin and that the reputation of those countries (as either backward or modern) depended on them.

The Business Model

In the beginning, work on *Woman and Home* was done in the Hansen family's home in the outskirts of Cedar Rapids, Iowa. The magazine was printed in town, but Ida Hansen and her sister Mina folded, sewed, and addressed the magazines by hand at home. As its popularity grew, the number of pages increased from eight plain text pages in 1888 to forty in 1901 with a vast number of advertisements and illustrations. Between 1888 and 1894, *Woman and Home*'s circulation rose from 1,000 to 15,000; by 1901, it had reached 70,000.[30] Ida Hansen gradually established a big and dedicated team of writers, coeditors, printers, and advertising employees, which included several family members. By 1903, the family had bought their own printing business in Cedar Rapids' town center and employed forty people. Two years later, the magazine had offices in Chicago, Minneapolis, and New York as well. In 1904, Ida and Niels Frederick Hansen moved to California, where they would live the rest of their lives. Probably the coeditors got a more important role after this, although Ida Hansen was listed as editor-in-chief until she died in 1938.[31]

One of the successful English-language women's magazines that Hansen had in mind when she launched *Women and Home* was undoubtedly the *Ladies' Home Journal*. This was the largest women's magazine in the United States at that time. It had been founded in 1883 by Mrs. Louisa Knapp Curtis, who served as the magazine's editor until 1889; it was the outgrowth of a column for women, edited by Knapp Curtis, that ran in her husband Cyrus Curtis's newspaper. Historian Helen Damon-Moore demonstrates how the Curtises, through their innovative work with advertising, established women as the new and most important consumers in the modern US society. The *Ladies' Home Journal* became a prototype for the ad-supported publishing business at the end of the nineteenth century.[32]

Woman and Home adopted several strategies used by the *Ladies' Home Journal,* such as encouraging its subscribers to read the ads carefully. It also ran editorials about the advertised products and offered several products as gifts to readers who drew in new subscribers. The message of both magazines was that in modern American families, women were in charge of the spending. These strategies worked for *Woman and Home.* By 1910, it had as many as eighteen pages of advertisements, and it had become one of the best advertising mediums among Scandinavian-American publications.[33]

Despite the similarities between *Woman and Home* and the *Ladies' Home Journal* in their design, gendered commercialism, and mix of traditional and modern values, there were clear differences. The *Ladies' Home Journal* contained less news and fewer editorials and readers' letters with progressive feminist content.[34] And, most important, the *Ladies' Home Journal* targeted white, English-speaking, middle-class women living in urban areas, whereas *Woman and Home* reached out to a more economically diverse and Scandinavian-American audience. Domestic servants and other employed women, farm women, and housewives in cities and towns subscribed to Hansen's magazine. To this audience of immigrant women, *Woman and Home* offered instruction on how to become important American consumers.

The editors of *Woman and Home* looked to a range of magazines and newspapers for inspiration, not just the *Ladies' Home Journal.*[35] They borrowed text and articles from the Norwegian progressive *New Ground* (*Nylænde*) and the more moderate *Urd,* from the Swedish *Idun,* from the American suffrage newspaper the *Woman's Journal,* and from several other American and Scandinavian newspapers, as well as from the *Ladies' Home Journal.*[36] The extracts regularly appeared in the column "For and About Women" ("For og om Kvinder") without attribution, as was the custom at the time. Clearly, the editors kept abreast of a variety of publications in an effort to keep themselves and their readers well informed.

Building an International Bridge

By implementing clever marketing strategies, *Woman and Home* attracted subscribers across a large geographic area. From the beginning, more copies than needed were printed and given to subscribers to pass along to friends or family members. Following the model from the *Ladies' Home Journal,* the magazine's subscribers were also rewarded with premiums for sending in names for new subscriptions. The higher the number of subscribers, the higher the value of the premiums. The best gifts were often knitting or sewing machines.[37] The various premiums were described in detail in the magazine, often with accompanying illustrations. The editors frequently asked for help in recruiting new subscribers, and the magazine's readers seem to have been happy to assist. Some sent letters with tips for others on how they succeeded in promoting subscriptions to others.

In the column "Our Letterbox," in April 1894, Mrs. Chr. Sørensen wrote that she had not previously been able to recruit subscribers because she "lived among [Anglo-] Americans." She had finally sent a subscription to Norway, and she encouraged others to do the same. She was convinced that *Woman and Home* would be "as dear a monthly guest at home as it is here" and that "many thoughts would come to mind that would not otherwise appear" when a relative or friend back home received the magazine as a loving greeting.[38]

Woman and Home was, however, far from the only US Scandinavian-language paper sent by immigrants to their friends and family back home. In studying the Norwegian immigrant press in the United States, Odd S. Lovoll found that Norwegian-American newspapers, especially in the weeks before Christmas, recommended a year's subscription as a perfect gift to send to Norway. Through such holiday gifts, many Norwegians became acquainted with Norwegian-American culture and with American culture and politics in general. According to Lovoll, these newspapers functioned as an international bridge. Historian Henrik Olav Mathiesen uses the term *transatlantic public sphere.*[39] This international bridge, or the transatlantic public sphere, was expanded by *Woman and Home* to include news for and about women. The magazine functioned as a cultural broker across the Atlantic.

Promoting Women's Independence

Ida Hansen took seriously her promise to include material on women's rights and "anything that can serve to promote women's independence."[40] Through the column "For and About Women," *Woman and Home*'s readers were kept up to date about women's issues. Most often, the column focused on women who had done something remarkable. Often, it presented news about political and societal changes that influenced women's situation. The material was taken from other newspapers and magazines and came mainly from Scandinavia and the United States but also from the rest of the world. The Anglo-American feminist newspaper the *Woman's Journal* may have served as an important source. It ran a similar column named "Concerning Women" and reported on politics and society elsewhere in the paper.[41]

"For and About Women" in the April 1894 issue of *Woman and Home* is representative of the column's usual content. In this particular issue, it covered twelve different pieces of news from around the world, with six updates from the United States, three from Scandinavia, and one each from France, Germany, and New Zealand. Five of the news items were about women who had accomplished something important in a field reflective of traditional gender roles—in these instances, a schoolteacher, a charity worker, a nurse, and a lacemaker. Two of the news stories were about women taking on untraditional roles. One noted that "Chicago now has 30 policewomen"; the other was about a woman who ran a pharmacy in Philadelphia. Of the five news items about societal change, one was about the founding of a new university for higher education for women in Weimar, Germany. The other four were about suffrage and political life. The editors wrote that women could soon get the right to vote in the French Chamber of Commerce and claimed that "if this law was passed, then there was no longer any reason to deny women the vote in municipal and parliamentary elections."[42] One item noted that women in Des Moines, Iowa, had been granted the right to vote in school and city elections; another mentioned that a woman in Norway, Anne Eggen, had been elected leader of the Liberal Party (Venstreforeningen) in Lom.

The fourth news item about suffrage, and the one that received the most thorough coverage, came from New Zealand. The previous September,

New Zealand had become the first self-governing country in the world to grant women the right to vote in parliamentary elections. The editors reproduced a report about the first election open to women that stated that "all negative prejudgments from the opponents of woman suffrage had been refuted." Women had organized in the cities and in the countryside to make sure that most women could vote. Women's committees took care of the children and other housekeeping jobs to make it possible for housewives to visit polling stations.[43] The story made it clear that women's domestic role was not threatened by their new ability to vote.

"For and About Women" was a regular column in *Woman and Home.* Every month, subscribers were introduced to strong, interesting role models who had succeeded in their fields. These individuals also embodied the concepts of individualism and freedom in American society. To many Norwegian women, emigration was a way to achieve freedom from the traditional way of life in Norway, which was characterized by a more authoritarian culture and strong family obligations.[44] Through the column, readers learned about the increasing opportunities for women and their political advancements in American and Scandinavian societies and beyond.

"The Good Wife" Paradox

Side by side with information in *Woman and Home* about women's progress and promotion of modern gender norms was material that explicitly encouraged readers to follow traditional nineteenth-century norms for women. For example, on the page after the "For and About Women" column in April 1894 was an article titled "The Good Wife." It advised women to put on a brave face and endure the hard work, humiliations, and injustices they would necessarily experience in their marriage and as housewives. The article ends with a poem conveying the following message: "Carry, learn, never feed the spark of strife with bitter words. Keep silent, endure, never claim your own rights with a high-tension string." In return, "domestic happiness will grow."[45] The juxtaposition of this advice and the news column about women's political and career achievements illustrates the double message that *Woman and Home* sent to its readers.

In fact, the space that *Woman and Home* devoted to progressive, feminist material was a small percentage of the magazine. A clear preponderance of the content revolved around traditional women's tasks within the private sphere. The editors apparently saw no contradiction in combining both types of material in one magazine. Or perhaps they did but did their best to avoid seeming to present two apparently opposite female role models. On several occasions, Ida Hansen reminded her readers that the magazine accepted all kinds of opinions. She claimed that everyone was entitled to have, and express, their own opinions on feminist matters like suffrage but that it should be done respectfully. She highlighted her aim to avoid conflict and promote inclusion. There could be many reasons for her inclusive strategy. An obvious one, of course, is a desire for commercial success.

Arguing for Political Rights

Side by side with ads for beauty and household products and tips about how to become good Scandinavian-American mothers and wives, *Woman and Home* ran columns arguing for women's rights and, especially, woman suffrage. The editors offered various arguments, some taken from Scandinavia, some from America, and some from the broad international stage. In presenting these arguments and in combining them, a meditation among different feminist norms and cultures was taking place.

In 1907, a note from the column "The Editors' Corner" proclaimed that women "here in America," even without the right to vote, were able "to participate in and exercise much influence on municipal life." This was evident, it was argued, by studying the donations made in 1907 by women in the United States. They totaled $23,062,400, of which two-thirds was given to charity and $4 million for educational purposes. The editors claimed that "this was proof that women wanted civil rights."[46] Scandinavian immigrant women could relate to this assertion. Fundraising and voluntary work were important parts of community life in the United States, not least in the new settlements. In most Scandinavian communities, women established women's clubs where this work was organized. For years, *Woman and Home* had offered women's clubs free advertising space, thereby encouraging their work and the organizing of women per se.

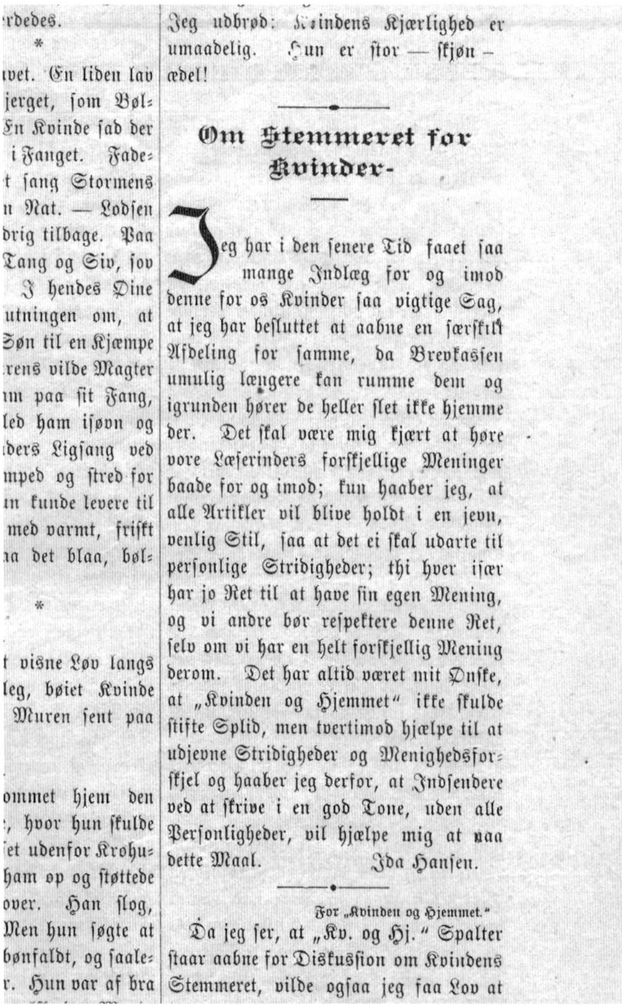

Jeg udbrød: K[illegible]indens Kjærlighed er umaadelig. Hun er stor — skjøn — ædel!

Om Stemmeret for Kvinder.

Jeg har i den senere Tid faaet saa mange Indlæg for og imod denne for os Kvinder saa vigtige Sag, at jeg har besluttet at aabne en særskilt Afdeling for samme, da Brevkassen umulig længere kan rumme dem og igrunden hører de heller slet ikke hjemme der. Det skal være mig kjært at høre vore Læserinders forskjellige Meninger baade for og imod; kun haaber jeg, at alle Artikler vil blive holdt i en jevn, venlig Stil, saa at det ei skal udarte til personlige Stridigheder; thi hver især har jo Ret til at have sin egen Mening, og vi andre bør respektere denne Ret, selv om vi har en helt forskjellig Mening derom. Det har altid været mit Ønske, at „Kvinden og Hjemmet" ikke skulde stifte Splid, men tvertimod hjælpe til at udjevne Stridigheder og Menighedsforskjel og haaber jeg derfor, at Indsendere ved at skrive i en god Tone, uden alle Personligheder, vil hjælpe mig at naa dette Maal.

Ida Hansen.

For „Kvinden og Hjemmet."

Da jeg ser, at „Kv. og Hj." Spalter staar aabne for Diskussion om Kvindens Stemmeret, vilde ogsaa jeg faa Lov at

Figure 4. The column "On Woman Suffrage" was launched in Winter 1893. *Woman and Home*, February 1893, 51. Image courtesy of Vesterheim Norwegian-American Museum, Decorah, Iowa.

As historian Sara Egge demonstrates, in the Midwest, where the majority of Norwegian Americans lived, both Anglo-American and immigrant women played vital roles building churches and other community institutions. Women raised money by selling homemade products at bazaars and organizing dinners. By taking an active part in community-building in this way, women demonstrated their social commitment. They performed their civic duty without stepping out of their domestic role. Strong opposition to woman suffrage and feminism existed in Midwestern communities. Therefore, women's participation in civic life through these fundraising activities was important to the eventual acceptance of woman suffrage, Egge contends.[47] *Woman and Home*'s argument that women's fundraising abilities proved that they deserved the right to vote echoed the strategy adopted by Anglo-American suffragists in the Midwest at the end of the nineteenth century.

Some years earlier, *Woman and Home* introduced readers to the Sámi woman Elsa Laula and her efforts to save the Indigenous community in Sweden and Norway. The editors presented Elsa Laula as an inspirational role model for courageously agitating for Sámi rights to Swedish and Norwegian authorities.[48] They wrote favorably about the Sámi population in northern Scandinavia and compared their situation to that of the Native Americans in the United States. This way of promoting feminism by using Elsa Laula and the Sámi people resembles that made earlier by American activists for woman suffrage. They had early on offered Native American nations as role models for Anglo-Americans seeking a more gender-equal society.[49]

At the end of the nineteenth century, influential US feminists adopted a different attitude toward Native Americans. Instead of seeing their culture as an inspiration to the cause, the enfranchisement of Native Americans was considered a threat and a potential impediment to Anglo-American women's own development.[50] *Woman and Home,* however, continued to present Native Americans as role models. In January 1918, the "For and About Women" column printed a notice reporting that the women among the "Delaware Indians" had the right to vote "since time immemorial" and that their women's council had won many important victories within the nation.[51]

Another tactic that the editors used when arguing for woman suffrage was to underline the advances already made. In the November 1894 issue, they presented an overview of voting rights laws around the world and began by proclaiming: "In quite a few of the world's countries, women already have the right to vote, but in most cases, this is limited to more local elections." They then listed where and in which types of elections women could vote. They stated that in New Zealand, as well as in Iceland, on the Isle of Man, and on the Pitcairn Islands, "women have full voting rights." This was not entirely accurate—some marital and income restrictions applied—but women in these places did have more political rights than most women in the United States.[52]

The only state in the United States where women had the same voting rights as men was Wyoming, which had enfranchised women in 1869. American women nonetheless could vote in a variety of elections in many other states. As the editors explained, "Here in the United States, women have the right to vote in 28 states and territories, and approximately 50,000 exercised this right in 1890."[53] These numbers were not inflated. Recent studies have shown that, before 1900, school boards in twenty-six states had provided women with voting rights, and in forty-three they could run for school boards. In the states where most Norwegian immigrants lived, suffrage varied. Minnesota had given women voting rights in school elections in 1875. Dakota Territory followed suit in 1879 and Wisconsin in 1886. Washington followed in 1890 (after various earlier efforts), Illinois in 1891, and Iowa in 1894.[54]

The editors concluded their overview by noting that women in Norway had the right to vote on school matters.[55] They were referring to the new Norwegian School Act (Lov om Folkeskolen paa Landet) that was passed in the country in 1889 and gave women this right.[56] The right to vote in school governance elections thus appears to have been something many Norwegian immigrant women had some awareness of from their old or new homeland.

"On Woman Suffrage"

In the February 1893 issue, Ida Hansen announced that she was launching a section of the magazine dedicated to woman suffrage. She reasoned that many readers were interested in the matter, writing about it in their letters to the magazine, both in favor and in opposition. The 1890s was a decade of increasing mobilization for woman suffrage in the Midwest. South Dakota advocates had organized a suffrage amendment campaign in 1890, and activists in Minnesota collected signatures for petitions. In 1891, the Minnesota Senate voted for a woman suffrage bill, although it later failed in the House. In Iowa, the suffrage movement intensified its efforts at local organizations and would soon experience a victory with the granting of partial suffrage to women in 1894.[57] These efforts must have inspired the readers of *Woman and Home*. In their everyday immigrant lives, they observed how notions of modernity and progress and female roles were negotiated in Anglo-American culture. To have the opportunity to express their own thoughts to others of Scandinavian background was clearly important to many. This negotiation in the pages of *Woman and Home* became a part of a continual identity-formation process among several generations of readers.

Hansen explained how the column "Our Letterbox" had become filled with letters from readers offering their opinions on woman suffrage. She encouraged readers to continue sharing their thoughts, which would now be included in the new column "On Woman Suffrage." She underlined that all readers were entitled to their own opinions. She only asked that all letters be written in "a friendly manner so that [the discussions] would not develop into personal disputes." Hansen concluded by stating that her wish was that the magazine not create discord but, on the contrary, help smooth out disputes and differences of opinion. She asked readers to help her achieve her goal by writing in a "polite way."[58]

The "On Woman Suffrage" column was short-lived, but the topic remained of interest to readers. The "Our Letterbox" column in the April 1894 issue ran a letter from Miss A. M. O. of Mekinock, North Dakota, that offers insights into the arguments for and against woman suffrage. She was responding to a letter in a previous issue from Helene in Saint Ansgar, Iowa, which had apparently been critical of woman suffrage: "[Helene] thinks that women have enough to do at home without bothering with politics, because as she says: 'if we were to vote we would have to read political magazines.' Well, this is possible! But [Helene] calls this: 'a waste of time.' I, for my part, think that every housewife should have enough time to spare to be able to read a little in the magazines. And yet, if she herself really has no time, her husband or other members of the family would have to give her the information she asked for on the matter."[59]

After refusing to accept the argument that women lack the time to learn about politics, A. M. O. stated that it is not strange that women do not understand politics since "their opinion is never sought, and whatever they might know or think, it would do just as much good, for they could not utter anything after all." She is convinced, she wrote, that if women had the right to vote, those who now claim not to care about politics would find joy in the subject because they would learn that it is useful and necessary for many reasons. Miss A. M. O. did not consider the home or the household to be threatened by or in conflict with woman suffrage, although she admitted that some think they are. She concluded by urging *Woman and Home* to continue accepting letters about woman suffrage.[60]

The Anglo-American suffragists' mobilization in the Midwest affected the magazine's readers and led to an increased interest for woman suffrage among Scandinavian immigrant women. This interest was further increased by Ida Hansen's invitation to discuss the topic in the magazine.

"The Small Community That We Call Home"

In the October issue for 1907, the magazine's peak year, the editors introduced a new monthly competition in place of the usual column of readers' letters, as the number of letters they had received was enormous.[61] They offered a prize for the best answer to the question "Which of the following social movements do you consider to be of greatest importance for women and homes of the future: the youth movement, the women's movement, the labor movement, or the temperance movement?" The magazine's January 1908 issue announced two winners and published their responses. Both winners had chosen the women's movement as the most important. The editors stated that it had been difficult to choose the best since there had been so many good and nearly identical answers.[62]

The first prize (two dollars) went to Mrs. Maria Refling of Douglas, Alaska. Refling began her answer proclaiming that "woman by becoming fully equal to man" would awaken to more self-confidence, higher development, and "a warmer interest in people and country." She also brought religious faith into her argument: "And, if life is to become what the all-knowing God has determined it to be, then man and woman must work together, give the best in themselves to the small community that we call home, as well as to the great community: the nation."[63] If women achieved equal rights, they could work to improve both home and country and thus help fulfill God's plan, she believed.

Although they did not discuss religion in the magazine, the editors knew very well that it played a fundamental role in the lives of most of their readers.[64] Many readers' letters expressed the importance of their faith, particularly when they felt lost in their new country and needed comfort. In the United States, religion and church life took on special roles for the immigrants. The church became both the religious and the cultural center of their communities. Norwegian Americans alone established several different denominations, most of them Lutheran, with the Norwegian Synod being the largest.[65]

The second prize (one dollar) was awarded to Mrs. I. Erickson of Washington. She declared that the women's movement was the most important, with temperance coming in second. Her main argument was that women, "more than any man," would contribute to the good of society if they were just given the opportunity. She saw the liberation of women as vital to them to be good mothers and educators of their children. It was also a prerequisite for the carrying out of other important reforms: "So long as the sensible and thinking woman shall be content to keep silent, merely because she is a woman, then sons and daughters often leave the home and go out into life with completely depraved characters, and the temperance work, as well as all other good reforms, becomes difficult to carry out. May God bless the work of temperance among drunkards; but what is sown in a child's heart takes the deepest roots."[66] Drunkenness was seen as a huge problem at the time, and many readers expressed their support for the temperance movement. The Women's Christian Temperance Union (WCTU), which became one of the largest reform movements in the United States during the late nineteenth and early twentieth centuries, promoted suffrage zealously. Frances Willard, its president, argued that since it was women's responsibility to protect their homes from the evils of alcohol, they should have the vote.[67] Some scholars believe that the temperance movement, or the WCTU, was the most common way for Scandinavian-American women to get involved in the suffrage movement.[68] Still, temperance was controversial and the link between the temperance movement and woman suffrage was not unambiguously positive. It led antiprohibitionists to oppose allowing women to vote.[69]

The contest question juxtaposed the words *women* and *home,* and in this way, it of course led the competition's participants to do the same. However, the winning answers, which the editors claimed were representative, indicate that, for several women, the most important reason that women should have more rights was that they would then be better housewives and educators of children. This finding accords with those of researchers of Scandinavian immigrant women in turn-of-the-nineteenth-century America. According to Gracia Grindal, the same arguments were used to explain the importance of building the Red Wing Ladies' Seminary for Norwegian-American girls in the 1890s. The Lutheran founders proclaimed the school's goal was to educate young girls to be good wives and mothers.[70]

A Feminism of Its Own?

Feminists in Norway began organizing formally in 1884, just four years before Ida Hansen began publishing *Woman and Home*. Before the 1880s, there were only two known feminists in Norway: the writer Camilla Collett and the painter and writer Aasta Hansteen. Hansteen became the first woman in Norway to publicly advocate for women's rights.[71] Feminists in the United States, in contrast, had already had decades of experience with feminist organizing. The first women's rights convention in Seneca Falls, New York, was held in 1848, forty years before Ida Hansen started her magazine. Norwegian feminists were inspired by these North American forerunners. For example, Hansteen wrote about American feminism for Norwegian papers.[72]

Aasta Hansteen had herself been an immigrant in the United States. During her sojourn in the United States from 1880 to 1889, she published in Norwegian-American newspapers and gave lectures on feminism to Scandinavian Americans in Chicago and Minneapolis. Hansteen also wrote for the Anglo-American feminist paper the *Woman's Journal,* which was published in Boston where she lived during most of her time in America.[73] In spite of this and the editors' seeming interest in informing readers about as many feminist role models as possible, *Woman and Home* barely mentioned Hansteen. The explanation for this omission may perhaps be found somewhere between the magazine's feminist and business strategies and the new strategy of the Anglo-American suffragists.

As stated previously, Hansen insisted on inclusivity and accepting everyone's opinion. She wanted the exchange of ideas to be polite and to avoid disputes. Hansteen, in contrast, did not avoid conflict. During her years in the

Figure 5. Norwegian feminist Aasta Hansteen, circa 1887–1890. Photographer unknown. Courtesy of the Oslo Museum.

United States, she attacked Norwegian Synod pastors in an article in the *Woman's Journal,* charging that they treated married women as "slaves." Hansteen also criticized her compatriots in the Midwest for backwardness, especially when it came to women's rights.[74] Such criticisms were risky. When Hansteen's acquaintances and fellow progressive Norwegian reformers—poet Bjørnstjerne Bjørnson, Unitarian pastor Kristofer Janson, and Marcus Thrane, Norway's first socialist leader—also criticized the Synod for backwardness and for oppressing women, they were labeled "freethinkers" and enemies of the Lutheran church and the prevailing order.[75]

Hansen had a business to protect and her own feminist mission to achieve. She could not jeopardize either by writing about matters that might cause a significant segment of her readers to lose faith in her project. Perhaps

Hansen admired Hansteen and would have liked to write about her earlier. She was in any case indebted to Hansteen for preparing the ground for feminists in Norway. But Hansen, a shrewd businesswoman and tactician, no doubt decided it was best to set Hansteen aside for the time being. In any case, she found more convenient arguments in the new American feminist discourse at the beginning of the twentieth century.

The first-generation Anglo-American feminists argued for women's rights and woman suffrage as natural rights, based on the concept that women were equal to men and therefore should have the same opportunities. This was also the argument that the first Norwegian women's rights advocates adopted. However, decades after the Seneca Falls Convention, during which Anglo-American suffragists worked hard but won few victories, the National American Woman Suffrage Association introduced a new argument around 1900. This has become known as the essentialist or expediency argument. Instead of focusing on a common humanity that includes men and women, as the natural rights argument did, it centered on how the two genders supposedly differed from each other. The argument was thus rooted in the Victorian public-and-private-spheres dichotomy. The new suffragist claim was that if women were given the right to vote, their inherent virtues, such as piety and purity, would lead them to seek, through the ballot, to improve society. Suffrage thus became linked to "municipal housekeeping."[76]

This argument was adapted to fit the Anglo-American ideal of women's domesticity. It made woman suffrage seem less threatening to family life. It may also have been more appealing to Scandinavian-American women, as it could be adapted to the limits and possibilities of the complementary identities of immigrant women. Feminism was entangled with immigrants' desire to succeed in their new homeland. Adapting to Anglo-American gender norms was an obvious part of this. As Donna Gabaccia demonstrates, immigrant women in the late nineteenth century understood that they needed to pursue exclusively domestic lives if they were to be accepted as proper Americans.[77]

The deradicalizing shift in the Anglo-American suffrage movement occurred at the same time as frustrations over mass immigration spurred nativist sentiment among the general Anglo-American population. The native-born suffragists considered immigrants to be backward and anti-suffragist. Scandinavian-American immigrant women understood this. They were more fortunate than other immigrant groups as they were considered to be near the top of the "whiteness" hierarchy and thus considered better able to adapt to Anglo-American values.[78] Norwegian Americans were nevertheless in general conservative and skeptical about feminism, as Hansteen pointed out.

Scandinavian-American women seeking to adopt the traditional role of the Anglo-American middle-class woman found *Woman and Home* to be a helpful mediator in the process. At the same time, the magazine became a medium where Scandinavian-American women could stay informed about developments with respect to women's issues in their new and old homelands and in the rest of the world. *Woman and Home* found arguments in favor of women's political rights in anything from modern Anglo-American news stories about economic success and charitable donations to non-Western Indigenous Peoples in both America and Scandinavia. The latter provided examples of alternative social organization and gender equality as well as role models of brave women who were taking part in political life and shaping the future of their nations.

As the number of subscribers to *Woman and Home* increased, the magazine's feminist message spread to a larger audience, one much bigger than any Hansteen was able to reach. As a cultural broker between conservative Scandinavian-American culture and Anglo-American feminist culture, Hansen enjoyed greater success than did Hansteen. *Woman and Home* may have shaped the outlook of generations of Scandinavian-American feminists with its careful packaging of feminism as supportive of rather than in conflict with the American ideal of domesticity.

Concluding Remarks

With *Woman and Home,* Ida Hansen created a communication medium dedicated to Scandinavian immigrant women. She also launched a successful business. Hansen's ambition was first and foremost to help immigrant women adjust to America, but at the same time she wanted to inform them of and promote women's rights. The magazine became a contact zone, an arena where different cultures and values met and were negotiated.

Hansen's aims, the magazine's editorial platform, and its business model reveal that *Woman and Home* was anything but a purely feminist publication. Instead, it closely resembled a typical ladies' magazine with most of its pages dedicated to housewives. This probably explains its success; its feminist message was packaged in a way that appealed to all kinds of immigrant women, not only radical and progressive ones. Through *Woman and Home,* thousands of Scandinavian immigrants stayed up to date on women's politics and feminist discussions. This made the magazine into an important advocate for women's rights and woman suffrage among Norwegian Americans.

The ways that the editors and readers of *Woman and Home* argued for women's rights demonstrates how different notions of feminism, womanhood, and femininity were negotiated and translated in the pages of the magazine. *Woman and Home* took on a role as a cultural broker between Scandinavian-American, Anglo-American, and Scandinavian cultures. Further, specific historical contexts influenced the construction of the arguments for women's rights and the way that norms and values were negotiated.

A striking feature of *Woman and Home* was the balance it struck between two opposite values—the modern and the traditional. At the same time that it told female readers to pursue traditional roles as mothers and housewives, it offered news about efforts to expand women's rights and opportunities. This paradoxical juxtaposition resonated with the arguments adopted by the Anglo-American suffrage movement after it deradicalized around the end of the nineteenth century. Still, the arguments in *Woman and Home* were shaped by Scandinavian Americans. Some of the magazine's content would have made little sense to an Anglo-American feminist audience with no roots in Scandinavia. Some content would also have made no sense to feminists in Norway. *Woman and Home* developed a feminism of its own.

Because of their complementary identity as immigrant women, Norwegian- and Scandinavian-American women embraced a feminism tailored to their own needs and circumstances. Their feminism was intertwined with their desire as immigrants to adjust to their new homeland and to be successful. To them, being modern and progressive meant something different than it did to the radical feminists back home in Norway. Scandinavian-American feminism necessarily had to adapt to the powerful Anglo-American middle-class ideal of domesticity. The editors and readers of *Woman and Home* wanted first and foremost for Scandinavian-American women to become modern American housewives, politically engaged and participating in civic life for the good of the home and the nation.

Mona Holm *is a PhD student in history at the University of Oslo and a curator at the Women's Museum in Norway. Her field of interest is women's history. Holm is the recipient of the 2023 NAHA Archives Fellowship.*

NOTES

1. *Kvinden og Hjemmet,* September 1918, 197, in Åse Elin Langeland, *Adjusting to America: A Study in Kvinden og Hjemmet: A Monthly Journal for the Scandinavian Women in America, 1888–1947* (VDM Verlag Dr. Müller, 2009), 14. The translation of this quote is from Åse Elin Langeland. I have read and used sampled issues of the magazine at the Rolvaag Special Collections at the St. Olaf College Library in Northfield, Minnesota, and the Vesterheim Museum Archives in Decorah, Iowa. In the endnotes, *Kvinden og Hjemmet* will hereafter be referred to as "*K&H.*" The article uses the magazine editors' English translation of the title (*Woman and Home*).
2. In 1905, the Chicago-based newspaper *Skandinaven* had a circulation of 48,335; in its most popular year, 1912, circulation had increased to nearly 54,000. Odd S. Lovoll, *Norwegian Newspapers in America: Connecting Norway and the New Land* (Minnesota Historical Society Press, 2010), 1, 139–40; Odd S. Lovoll, *The Promise of America: A History of the Norwegian-American People* (Universitetsforlaget, 1984), 122.
3. Jon Gjerde, *The Minds of the West: The Ethnocultural Evolution in the Rural Middle West, 1830–1917* (University of North Carolina Press, 1997), 8, 240.
4. Synnøve Skarsbø Lindtner, " 'Som en frisk vind gjennom stuen': Kvinnebladet 'Sirene' (1973–1983) og det utvidete politikkbegrepet" (PhD diss., University of Bergen, 2014), 126–28.
5. Anna M. Peterson's research on Scandinavian-American suffragists in the Midwest at the turn of the last century has been a major inspiration for this article. Anna M. Peterson, " 'A Dash of Suffrage Spice': Rural and Urban Ethnicity Construction in the Transnational Women's Suffrage Movement" (master's thesis, University of North Dakota, 2009); "Adding 'a Little Suffrage Spice to the Melting Pot': Minnesota's Scandinavian Woman Suffrage Association," *Minnesota History* 62, no. 8 (2011): 288–97, http://www.jstor.org/stable/23066829; "Making Women's Suffrage Support an Ethnic Duty: Norwegian American Identity Constructions and the Women's Suffrage Movement, 1880–1925,"

Journal of American Ethnic History 30, no. 4 (2011): 5–23, https://doi.org/10.5406/jamerethnhist.30.4.0005.

6. Donna Gabaccia, *From the Other Side: Women, Gender, and Immigrant Life in the U.S., 1820–1990* (Indiana University Press, 1994), 124, 127, 128.
7. I use the term *Anglo-American* in line with this definition from the *Merriam-Webster Dictionary*: "a North American whose native language is English and especially whose culture or ethnic background is of European origin." *Merriam-Webster Dictionary,* "Anglo-American," accessed 9 June 2025, https://www.merriam-webster.com/dictionary/Anglo-American.
8. Mary Louise Pratt, "Arts of the Contact Zone," *Profession* (1991): 33–40, http://www.jstor.org/stable/25595469.
9. Judith Becker, introduction to *European Missions in Contact Zones: Transformation Through Interaction in a (Post-)Colonial World,* ed. J. Becker (Vandenhoeck & Ruprecht, 2015).
10. Lovoll, *Promise of America,* 28.
11. Knud Langeland, *Nordmændene i Amerika* (1889), 94, cited in Lovoll, *Norwegian Newspapers in America,* 1.
12. According to Lovoll, all immigrant ethnic groups developed their own foreign-language presses. The most expansive period of the Norwegian-language press was the late 1870s to approximately 1910. Most papers did not last long, but some became stable institutions. Lovoll, *Norwegian Newspapers in America,* 93–94.
13. Swedish immigrant women, who outnumbered those from Norway and Denmark, got their own edition of the magazine, *Qvinnan och Hemmet,* in 1893. After this, the original *Woman and Home,* which had the widest readership, became dedicated mainly to a Dano-Norwegian audience. Åse Elin Langeland points out that, since there were more Norwegian immigrant women than Danish ones, the majority of subscribers were probably Norwegian. Note that the circulation numbers include both editions. Langeland, *Adjusting to America,* 11.
14. Hansen's grandfather, the farmer Lars Jensen (1784–1852), had been an innovative educator and, in addition to teaching, had founded a teacher-training course. He also served as a member of the Norwegian parliament. His belief in education must have been transmitted to later generations. Nancy L. Coleman, Eva-Marie Syversen, and Anne Kari Vasaasen, "Exploring the Scandinavian Woman with Ida and Mina," *Vesterheim* 21, no. 1 (2023): 11–19.
15. The translations of the title of this newspaper and its column, as well as of the various columns of *Woman and Home,* are from Langeland, *Adjusting to America.*
16. Langeland, *Adjusting to America,* 14–22; Coleman et al., "Exploring the Scandinavian Woman," 11–19.
17. *K&H,* June 1888, 15.
18. Lovoll, *Promised Land,* 36, 54, 80–86, 153; Ingrid Semmingsen, "Kvinner i norsk utvandringshistorie," *Migranten: The Migrant* 1 (1988): 7–10.
19. "In Memoriam N.Fr. Hansen," *K&H,* October 1935. All translations are mine if not otherwise stated.
20. "In Memoriam N.Fr. Hansen."
21. Langeland, *Adjusting to America,* 16. N.Fr. Hansen, who was Danish, came from Schleswig, which in 1869 had become part of Prussia (later Germany).

22. *K&H,* February 1918, 28.
23. *K&H,* May 1888, 1.
24. The transition into middle-class Anglo-American gender norms naturally varied. L. DeAne Lagerquist, *In America the Men Milk the Cows* (Carlson, 1991), 58–59, 102–3; Lori Ann Lahlum, "Women, Work, and Community in Rural Norwegian America, 1840–1920," in *Norwegian American Women: Migration, Communities, and Identities,* ed. Betty A. Bergland and Lori Ann Lahlum (Minnesota Historical Society Press, 2011), 84–86.
25. *K&H,* May 1888, 1.
26. *K&H,* May 1888, 1.
27. *K&H,* May 1888, 1.
28. *K&H,* May 1888, 1.
29. For a discussion of how the term *Norwegian Americans* came into use, see Daron W. Olson, *Vikings Across the Atlantic: Emigration and the Building of a Greater Norway, 1860–1945* (University of Minnesota Press, 2013), 31, 237.
30. The number was large throughout the first decades of the 1900s, with 70,000 in 1901 and 60,000 in 1924. In 1896, an English version, *Woman and Home,* began publication. This edition targeted younger generations of Scandinavian Americans who knew English better than the Dano-Norwegian language. Despite reaching as many as 10,000 copies, this magazine was sold after only one year. Langeland, *Adjusting to America,* 17–19; *K&H,* December 1937.
31. Langeland, *Adjusting to America,* 14–20, 26–27; " 'Kvinden og Hjemmet' Feirer 50 Aars Jubilæum," *K&H,* December 1937.
32. Helen Damon-Moore, *Magazines for the Millions: Gender and Commerce in the "Ladies' Home Journal" and the "Saturday Evening Post," 1880–1910* (State University of New York Press, 1994), 2–8.
33. Langeland, *Adjusting to America,* 17–19; " 'Kvinden og Hjemmet.' "
34. Some issues of the *Ladies' Home Journal* from the period during which Mrs. Louisa Knapp Curtis was editor (1883–1889) are digitally available at "Ladies' Home Journal and Practical Housekeeper," HathiTrust, https://catalog.hathitrust.org/Record/000059805. A selection of issues has been quickly revised, and one targeted digital search on the word *suffrage* (a word frequently used in *Woman and Home*) led to just four hits for the years 1885–1889 (May 1885, 13; November 1887, 2; October 1887, 2; April 1887, 17). All accessed 31 December 2024.
35. *Urd,* which was launched in 1897 in Norway by another pair of sisters, Anna and Cecilie Bøe, is the magazine in Norway most akin to *Woman and Home. Urd* advocated progress and enlightenment while at the same time defending and cultivating traditional female roles and values. It is not surprising that *Woman and Home* often published material from this magazine. Yet *Woman and Home* was launched almost a decade before *Urd* and may have inspired the Norwegian magazine. *Woman and Home* journalist Ingeborg Rasmussen also wrote for *Urd.*
36. Lindtner, " 'Som en frisk vind gjennom stuen,' " 122–23. See Lindtner for an overview of the history of women's magazines in Norway.
37. Langeland, *Adjusting to America,* 17; various issues of *K&H.*
38. *K&H,* April 1894, 88.
39. Lovoll, *Norwegian Newspapers in America,* 211–13; Henrik Olav Mathiesen, "The

Epistolary Practices of Norwegian Emigrants and the Emergence of a Transatlantic Public Sphere, ca. 1835–1870" (PhD diss., University of Oslo, 2021).

40. *K&H,* May 1888, 1.
41. See, for example, *Woman's Journal,* January 1881, 1, available at "Woman's Journal, 1881," Schlesinger Library, Radcliffe Institute, Harvard University, Cambridge, MA, accessed 31 December 2024, https://iiif.lib.harvard.edu/manifests/view/drs:48874700$7i.
42. *K&H,* April 1894, 74–75.
43. *K&H,* April 1894, 74–75.
44. During the early nineteenth century, new social networks replaced the traditional ones in the United States. See, for example, Paul Boyer et al., *The Enduring Vision: A History of the American People,* 7th ed. (2009; Wadsworth Cengage Learning, 2013), 214.
45. *K&H,* April 1894, 76. Original text: "Bære, lære, aldrig nære Stridens gnist med bitre Ord. Tie, Taale, aldrig Maale egen Ret med høispent Snor—Deraf huslig lykke gror."
46. *K&H,* August 1907, 304.
47. Sara Egge, *Woman Suffrage and Citizenship in the Midwest, 1870–1920* (Iowa Press, 2018), 18–25, 38–41.
48. *K&H,* July 1904, 197; *K&H,* January 1905, 7–8. For more on Elsa Laula Renberg (her name after marrying), see Siri Broch Johansen, *Elsa Laula Renberg: Historien om samefolkets store Minerva* (CálliidLágádus, 2015).
49. Sally Roesch Wagner, "How Native American Women Inspired the Women's Rights Movement," Belmont-Paul Women's Equality National Monument, Women's Rights National Historical Park, April 17, 2020, https://www.nps.gov/articles/000/how-native-american-women-inspired-the-women-s-rights-movement.htm; Gail H. Landsman, "The 'Other' as Political Symbol: Images of Indians in the Woman Suffrage Movement," *Ethnohistory* 39, no. 3 (1992): 247–84, https://www.jstor.org/stable/482299.
50. Egge, *Woman Suffrage and Citizenship,* 101.
51. *K&H,* January 1918, 19. The source referred to is probably Richard Calmit Adams, *A Brief History of the Delaware Indians* (US Government Printing Office, 1906).
52. *K&H,* November 1894, 247–48; "Celebrating Women's Suffrage in the Isle of Man," Tynwald: Parliament of the Isle of Man, 24 September 2018, https://tynwald.org.im/news/celebrating-womens-suffrage-in-the-isle-of-man; Auður Styrkársdóttir, "Women's Suffrage in Iceland," Women's History Archives, 2006, https://kvennasogusafn.is/index.php?page=Womens-Suffrage-in-Iceland; "Women and the Vote: Page 5–World Suffrage Timeline," New Zealand History, updated 27 April 2023, https://nzhistory.govt.nz/politics/womens-suffrage/world-suffrage-timeline.
53. *K&H,* November 1894, 247–48.
54. Kathryn A. Nicholas, "Reexamining Women's Nineteenth-Century Political Agency: School Suffrage and Office-Holding," *Journal of Policy History* 30, no. 3 (2018): 452, 463–67, Table 1, https://doi.org/10.1017/S0898030618000179.
55. *K&H,* November 1894, 247–48.
56. *Nylænde,* 1 July 1893, 175.
57. Egge, *Woman Suffrage and Citizenship,* 81–93; "Women's Suffrage in Iowa," Iowa State University Carrie Chapman Catt Center for Women and Politics, accessed 14 April 2025, https://cattcenter.iastate.edu/timeline/.

58. *K&H,* February 1893, 51–53. The cover of this issue is missing, but the year can be determined due to the dating of one of the readers' letters on page 52.
59. *K&H,* April 1894, 88.
60. *K&H,* April 1894, 88.
61. Langeland, *Adjusting to America,* 24.
62. *K&H,* January 1908, 24.
63. *K&H,* January 1908, 24.
64. For an overview of how *Woman and Home* covered Christian faith, see Langeland, *Adjusting to America,* 59–64. Her assessment, however, differs slightly from my own. According to her, Christian faith was given greater space than I have observed.
65. Ralph Meier, "Norwegian-American Lutheran Identity in America Until 1917: The Norwegian Synod, Its Affiliations with the Missouri Synod, and Doctrinal Controversies," in *Norwegian-American Essays 2020: Migration, Minorities and Freedom of Religion,* ed. Terje Mikael Hasle Joranger and Harry Cleven (Novus Press, 2020), 91.
66. *K&H,* January 1908, 24.
67. Egge, *Woman Suffrage and Citizenship,* 65–66.
68. Gracia Grindal, *Unstoppable: Norwegian Pioneers Educate Their Daughters* (Lutheran University Press, 2016), 323.
69. Egge, *Woman Suffrage and Citizenship,* 122–23.
70. Grindal, *Unstoppable,* 265, 280 (and the whole book).
71. See Anna Caspari Agerholt, *Den norske kvinnebevegelses historie* (1937; Gyldendal, 1973); Aslaug Moksnes, *Likestilling eller særstilling? Norsk kvinnesaksforening 1884–1913* (Gyldendal, 1984); Hilde Danielsen, Eirinn Larsen, and Ingeborg W. Owesen, *Norsk likestillingshistorie 1814–2013* (Fagbokforlaget Vigmostad og Bjørke, 2015). All of these have been formative for Norwegian historiography on the rise of feminism in Norway.
72. Mona Holm, "Living the American Dream: Re-Imagining Aasta Hansteen as a Norwegian Feminist Figure" (forthcoming); "The Nineteenth Amendment: The Fight for Women's Suffrage as Seen Through 'The Woman Citizen,' " UC Berkeley Library, accessed 26 November 2024, https://exhibits.lib.berkeley.edu/spotlight/women-vote/feature/the-woman-citizen.
73. Holm, "Living the American Dream"; "Nineteenth Amendment."
74. *Woman's Journal,* 30 July 1881, 244–45.
75. Janson and Thrane lived several years among Norwegian Americans, while Bjørnson was visiting in 1880–1881. Olson, *Vikings Across the Atlantic,* 64; Grindal, *Unstoppable,* 246, 250; Holm, "Living the American Dream."
76. Egge, *Woman Suffrage and Citizenship,* 120; Landsman, " 'Other' as Political Symbol," 253–54.
77. Gabaccia, *From the Other Side,* 115.
78. Erika K. Jackson, *Scandinavians in Chicago: The Origin of White Privilege in Modern America* (University of Illinois Press, 2019); Terje Mikael Hasle Joranger, "Ideal Immigrants? Ethnic Community Building Among Norwegian Americans in the Nineteenth Century," in *Nordic Whiteness and Migration to the USA: A Historical Exploration of Identity,* ed. Jana Sverdljuk et al. (Routledge, 2020).

Remembering Capt. Robert M. Losey, Killed by the Nazis in Norway Eighty-Five Years Ago, the First American Military Casualty in WWII

Gary G. Yerkey

It was the kind of wonderful winter-spring day that we have in Norway in April. There is a good smell from the melting snow, a fragrance of pine needles [and] of moss and wet earth wherever a stony mound juts up out of the snow. . . . And then the American military attaché, Captain Losey, was killed.

—SIGRID UNDSET, NORWEGIAN NOVELIST AND WINNER OF THE 1928 NOBEL PRIZE FOR LITERATURE

On the morning of 9 April 1940, Florence Jaffray "Daisy" Harriman, the American minister to Norway, sent an urgent message to her boss in Washington, DC, US Secretary of State Cordell Hull, saying that German military forces were invading neutral Norway, exclaiming almost incredulously in a secret cable that Norway was now "at war with Germany!"[1]

Earlier, Harriman had been awakened by a telephone call from the British minister to Norway, Sir Cecil Dormer, who said that a fleet of warships had been seen steaming up the fjord toward Oslo.

A short time later, Norwegian Foreign Minister Halvdan Koht called Harriman and confirmed that the ships were indeed German, adding that the Norwegian government, along with King Haakon VII, his thirty-six-year-old son (Crown Prince Olav), and the Royal Court would be leaving shortly by train for Hamar. Koht hoped that Harriman would be able to join them.

But Harriman was unable to make the train on such short notice, and instead, at 9:45 a.m., the sixty-nine-year-old diplomat and three staff members from the Legation piled into her 1937 Ford V-8 and followed a procession of vehicles steadily streaming out of town—hoping to catch up with the King and company at some point.

"In my trusty Ford were more suitcases than seemed possible," Harriman recalled in her memoir, *Mission to the North,* published in 1941. "As we approached Lilleström, on the outskirts of Oslo, we could hear the snap, snap, snap of machine guns overhead. A small Norwegian plane was giving chase to a Heinkel—we craned to watch. Drivers pressed forward, not exactly frightened, but we all breathed easier, as we moved out from under those dark outlines of the sky. Only one car, the third ahead of us, was struck by falling shrapnel. No one was hurt, but dents and scraped paint were sharp reminders of how narrow the escapes were."[2]

The Nazis were clearly on the march, having invaded Poland in September 1939, starting what would become a world war lasting some six years. Also in April, they invaded Norway's Nordic neighbor Denmark—followed by Belgium, the Netherlands, Luxembourg, and France a month later.

As Harriman was heading north from Oslo in her "trusty," chauffeur-driven Ford, her counterpart in Sweden, Frederick A. Sterling, was also in contact with Secretary Hull, saying that he had been unable to reach Harriman or the Legation in Oslo because telephone communications with Norway had been cut off.

Hull, therefore, instructed Sterling to send Capt. Robert M. Losey, a military attaché at the Legation, to Norway as soon as possible to assist in the evacuation of Harriman and other US diplomatic personnel and their families.

Prior to being sent to Sweden, Losey was posted to Finland, serving as air and assistant military attaché at the American Legation in Helsinki. His assignment—as a trained aeronautical meteorologist—was to report on air-related developments in the ongoing Winter War between Finland and the Soviet Union, where the harsh winter conditions provided an opportunity to observe the interplay between meteorology and military aeronautics.

But as the Winter War wound down and the Germans were in the process of invading Norway, Losey was ordered to report to the American Legation in Sweden to be nearer to the action.[3]

A handsome and, by all accounts, brilliant young US Air Corps officer, Losey was born on 27 May 1908 in Andrew, Iowa, where his father, Leon, served as pastor at the First Presbyterian Church.

Later, the family moved east, settling in New York State, where Leon served at several Presbyterian churches and at one point worked with the Interchurch World Movement. In 1920, the family moved again—this time to Wyoming and then on to Terry, Montana, where on 8 July 1923, Leon died suddenly. After the funeral, his wife Nellie decided to relocate to New Jersey, her home state, along with the couple's two young children, Robert and Margaret.

In 1924, Losey graduated from Trenton High School in New Jersey, and a year later he entered the United States Military Academy at West Point. On graduation, in 1929, he was commissioned a second lieutenant in the field artillery. Three months later, he was transferred to the US Army Air Corps, and after completing primary and advanced flight school in 1930, he was assigned to the 77th Pursuit Squadron at Mather Field near Sacramento, California, and later to Barksdale Field in Louisiana.

Figure 1. Portrait of Robert Moffat Losey (1908–1940) from *The Howitzer: The Yearbook of the United States Corps of Cadets*, 1929. Courtesy of Wikimedia Commons.

In the spring of 1933, Losey married Kathryn Leona Gault "Kay" Banta—the daughter of a distinguished army surgeon. He went on to earn two master's degrees (one in meteorology and another in aeronautical engineering) at the California Institute of Technology in Pasadena, and in May 1935 he was assigned to March Field in Riverside, California, as a meteorology officer.

In June 1937, Losey was ordered to report to Washington, DC, to serve as the first chief of the Weather Service in the office of the Chief of Air Corps—a position he held until January 1940, when he handed the reins to Arthur Merewether (also a trained meteorologist) after Losey, now thirty-one years old, was named to be air and assistant military attaché at the US Legation in Helsinki.

In Finland, Losey wrote reports for the Air Corps on the performance of Soviet warplanes and other equipment that were being used in the Winter War between the Soviet Union and Finland, which ended with the signing of a peace agreement between the two countries in mid-March 1940.

Meanwhile, in April of that year, as Harriman and her party were continuing their flight from Oslo, about two dozen family members from the American Legation, including eight children, also departed the Norwegian capital and headed for neutral Sweden.

The party, led by Lt. Cmdr. Ole O. Hagen, the Legation's naval attaché, at first was forced to turn back due to a collapsed bridge, eventually ending up stuck in five feet of snow.

Rescued by a group of local Norwegian civilians, they spent the night at a hotel in a small town about thirty miles northeast of Oslo. From there, they continued north but were again halted by a collapsed bridge, this time near Ringsaker, where they were forced to abandon their cars and walk for two hours through a blinding blizzard before hitching a ride on a truck. On 15 April, they reached the tiny mountain village of Sjusjøen, Norway, a few miles to the north, where they settled in.

Unknown to the Hagen-led party, the Harriman contingent—with her Norwegian chauffeur, Lars M. Frøislie, at the wheel of her car—crossed the border into neutral Sweden without a problem on 12 April. "The Customs officer waved us through, and we were directed to a small pension at [the border town of] Höljes," Harriman recalled. "The little inn proved most comfortable. Its modern plumbing fixtures delighted us. . . . The bed was real!"

Her first order of business, however, was not to sleep but to contact Minister Sterling at the American Legation in Stockholm. "It had been three days since I had been able to report," she said, "and I knew that Washington was probably anxious to know that we were still alive."

Sterling told Harriman that Secretary of State Hull had instructed him to send Captain Losey to join her and that the young military officer would be arriving in Höljes, Sweden, around midnight. Too tired to stay up to greet him, she met him at breakfast the next morning. He was a "nice, spare young man in a flying corps uniform," Harriman wrote in her diary at the time, "and [he] seems in every way acceptable."

After breakfast, it was decided during what Harriman referred to, tongue in cheek, as an informal "council of war" that she, Losey, and Frøislie would head north with the aim of eventually locating the Hagen-led party of American evacuees.

At lunch later that day in Särna, Sweden, Losey said that he was ready to press on immediately back across the Norwegian border to Lillehammer, and so Harriman, who was anxious to know the exact whereabouts and welfare of the Hagen-led group, agreed that Losey and Frøislie should make the trip alone.

But the excursion was a failure. At Lillehammer, they found that the mountain road to Sjusjøen, where the Hagen-led party was holed up, was blocked with snow. Yet during the trip he was able to glean valuable military intelligence—the first of its kind by an American official—concerning, in particular, the movement of German and Norwegian troops.

The next day, Losey left by car for Stockholm to report on his findings to Sterling in person and others at the American Legation. He returned to Salen, Sweden, by train on the evening of 18 April, when at dinner he and Harriman decided to set off again for Lillehammer to find, as Harriman put it, "our own refugees."

As they traveled north—forced to take a more circuitous route north to Norway because the more direct road west to Lillehammer was closed—they discussed whether Harriman should accompany Losey to the strategic railway junction city of Dombås, Norway, which was being bombed by the Germans.

"You might be bombed," Losey told Harriman. "The Germans are strafing the roads."

"But so might you," Harriman replied, "and that would be worse for you are young and have your life before you, while I have had a wonderful life and nearly all of it behind me."

"I certainly don't want to be killed," Losey countered, "but your death would be more serious as it might involve our country in all kinds of trouble, whereas with a military attaché . . ."

Losey explained that, in a moving automobile, it was almost impossible to hear the sound of a bomber overhead if it approached from the rear.

"We argued about sounds," Harriman recalled. "He gave me such precise details of the dangers we might encounter that I began to chaff him about being nervous. . . . His final argument for my safety was that if he and the chauffeur [Frøislie] went on alone, they could travel day and night without stopping." I was loath to listen but told him I would make up my mind after luncheon."

Harriman wrote in her diary later that day—after informing Losey that she had decided to stay behind—that Losey "couldn't be nicer, he is so understanding and gentle. I am certainly in luck to have such an aide sent me."

"I hated to see him go," Harriman recalled, "but when he impressed on me that 'our first job must be to get those women out,' I knew that he was right."

The next day, with a first aid kit and some chocolates and biscuits, Losey and Frøislie headed north through Sweden in Harriman's Ford V-8—with an American flag tied to the top of the car to help ward off an attack by German bomber aircraft.

"I will cheer when they return," Harriman wrote in her diary that day.[4]

On 20 April, meanwhile, the Hagen-led group of American evacuees arrived safely in Dombås after more than a week on the road and took refuge in a railway tunnel while awaiting transportation to Brekken, near the Swedish border, about 130 miles to the northeast. From there, they took a short bus ride to the Swedish border town of Fjällnäs—and safety.

"I knew the area was becoming a dangerous fighting sector," Hagen later recalled, recounting the twelve-day adventure, "so I forced the party to keep going, although all were dog tired."[5]

By Saturday, 21 April, Losey and Frøislie—still unaware of the Hagen party's whereabouts—had made their way across the Swedish border to Oppdal, about thirty miles northeast of Dombås, where they learned that the road to Dombås was blocked with snow. So they put the car on a train and eventually arrived in Dombås around 3 p.m.

Later that day, Harriman received word that Hagen had brought the American evacuees—"our wives and children"—across the border to safety in neutral Sweden. But she was concerned about Losey. "Uneasy. No report from the Captain," she wrote in her diary that day.

In Dombås, meanwhile, Losey and Frøislie found a restaurant near the railway station and sat down to have a much-needed bite to eat.

After about an hour in the restaurant, Losey and Frøislie heard an air raid siren and ran toward a railway tunnel nearby that had been cut through rock. About eighty other people also took shelter in the tunnel, mostly civilians. Minutes later, they heard machine guns and antiaircraft weapons opening fire on several planes overhead.

Several days earlier, Colonel General (*Generaloberst*) Nikolaus von Falkenhorst—the commander of the German invasion forces in Norway—had been ordered by the German Armed Forces High Command (*Oberkommando der Wehrmacht*) to seize control of Dombås in response to a report, which turned out to be false, that British troops had landed at Åndalsnes, Norway, about sixty-five miles to the northeast.

The main objective of the German operation was to destroy the railway station in Dombås and to block any possible British advance inland, particularly to the south.

Eventually, Losey and Frøislie heard a plane above them that appeared to be leaving the area and thought that the raid was over.

Suddenly, however, a bomb exploded nearby, sending shrapnel straight at Losey, striking him in the chest and killing him instantly.

Word of Losey's death first came from a Maj. Yssum, presumably a Norwegian army officer, in Oppdal, who sent in a brief message to Minister Sterling at the American Legation in Stockholm later on 21 April.

"American Military Attaché Losey was killed by German bomber plane at Dombås today," the message read. "Inform Mrs. Harriman. He will be sent tomorrow, Monday, via Røros to Fjällnäs where instructions from Legation are awaited."

The next day, 22 April, Sterling called Harriman to inform her of the loss. "I have some terrible news," he said, pausing to let Harriman catch her breath. "Captain Losey was killed yesterday by a German bomb."

Harriman was shocked. "All day we had been expecting him," she said later. "Our sense of loss in the world was centered in that one young American."[6]

From Dombås, Losey's body was transported first by Harriman's car and eventually by horse-drawn sledge over steep mountain roads to the Swedish border town of Fjällnäs, where it was placed on a Swedish Army truck for Hede, about fifty miles southeast. From there, it was taken by train to Stockholm.

After a memorial service at a small chapel in Stockholm—attended by Harriman, Sterling, and diplomats from several countries, including Great Britain, France, Norway, and Finland—Losey's body was cremated, and his ashes were returned by ship to the United States, where they were interred during a funeral service at the US Military Academy at West Point on 29 May.

Attending the service was Losey's wife, Kay, who earlier, on hearing that her husband had been killed, was quoted as saying, "It's a war and I guess you can expect anything." And then she collapsed.[7]

Harriman, for her part, wrote later that she had known Losey for only a few weeks but that she had seen "what his character was, and as taps were sounded [at the memorial service in Stockholm], it seemed as if I had lost a son."

She said that her heart also ached for the young widow in California who would now have to go on without him.

"She would be hearing [journalist Arthur Menken] on the radio [in the United States] telling of the service [in Stockholm]; she would read the beautiful tributes to him in the American press; she would not have the picture of the friends . . . who mourned him in the north."[8]

If she were alive today, Losey's widow would be able to view a simple stone monument in Dombås honoring her husband's memory, unveiled in a small park adjacent to the village church in 1987.

An inscription on the monument (the brainchild of the then-US ambassador to Norway Mark Evans Austad, who served from 1982 to 1984) reads:

IN

MEMORY OF

CAPTAIN ROBERT LOSEY USAAC

KILLED IN ACTION AT DOMBÅS

21ST APRIL

THE FIRST AMERICAN SERVICEMAN

TO GIVE HIS LIFE FOR HIS

COUNTRY IN WORLD WAR II

ALSO

IN MEMORY OF THE MANY

AMERICAN SERVICEMEN WHO LATER

IN THE WAR LOST THEIR LIVES

IN NORWAY WHILE FIGHTING

FOR THE LIBERATION OF

THIS COUNTRY

Figure 2. Dombås war memorial, Robert Losey. Courtesy of Wikimedia Commons.

On 21 April 1990, to mark the fiftieth anniversary of Losey's death, then-US ambassador to Norway Loret Miller Ruppe visited Dombås.

Speaking at a ceremony at the stone monument, she said that she had come to Dombås to honor the twenty-nine Norwegians who had lost their lives defending the region in the spring of 1940 and to remember the suffering of the area residents during the five years of German occupation.

Ruppe said that she had also come to Dombås to commemorate the death of Losey—"the first American serviceman in the uniform of his country to die in the Second World War."

She also suggested that, in fact, Losey had left the railway tunnel in Dombås before being struck by shrapnel, saying that he did not have to expose himself to the danger of the German bombs but chose "to move away from the protection of the wall of the tunnel in order to better observe the enemy's tactics and weapons of war." In an instant, she said, he was dead.

"A human heart can be pierced by shrapnel, or bullets or bombs, but the heart beat of a people can never be destroyed," Ruppe said. "The heart and spirit of the Norwegian people and the American people survived and prevailed, and we feel that heart and spirit as we stand here today."

Ruppe also quoted President Franklin D. Roosevelt, who said in September 1942 that if there were still people who were wondering why the United States was fighting the war, "look to Norway."

"If there is anyone who has any delusions that this war could have been averted," Ruppe quoted Roosevelt as saying, "look to Norway. And if there is anyone who doubts the democratic will to win, again I say, let him look to Norway."[9]

It might be said that after the United States entered the war in December 1941, President Roosevelt himself would "look to Norway"—overseeing US military operations against Nazi targets in occupied Norway, as well as clandestine operations in support of the anti-Nazi resistance movement through a Stockholm Office of Strategic Services (OSS) outpost—the immediate predecessor of the CIA—which was established by Roosevelt in June 1942.

Over the course of the war, OSS Stockholm personnel worked with Norwegian resistance groups north of the sixty-second parallel (so as not to interfere with similar British operations in the south) from several makeshift bases located just over the Norwegian border inside Sweden, supplying weapons and explosives for sabotage missions that would eventually undermine German military operations.

One such operation targeted railroad lines that were used by German troops; another involved the demolition of a Nazi regimental supply depot filled with highway construction machinery and other equipment.

Providing crucial logistic support to OSS Stockholm was an air unit run by the Norwegian-born American Arctic explorer and pioneering aviator Bernt Balchen, which, among other things, would drop hundreds of tons of weapons, ammunition, explosives, food, and medicine to Norwegian resistance fighters on the ground.

From 1941 to 1943, Balchen had commanded an air base in Greenland (Bluie West-8) that was used as a staging station for US aircraft being ferried to Europe. While there, he rescued downed American airmen and destroyed the only German outpost on the island.

But his real interest was in doing whatever he could to help drive the Nazis out of his native Norway, so he asked Gen. Henry H. Arnold, commander of the US Army Air Forces, to send him to Europe, and by early 1944 he had set up shop at Stockholm's Bromma Airport.

Over the next few months, Balchen created his own air force of some sixty airplanes, and soon—in June 1944—he was at the controls of one of his B-24s headed for Norway with three and a half tons of weapons and explosives to be used by the Norwegian resistance fighters in an upcoming sabotage operation against a Nazi heavy-water plant.

Near the target, three bonfires that had been set by the resistance's reception committee guided the B-24 toward its target, and twelve containers were quickly unloaded for use by the brave men on the ground.

Occasionally, Balchen's fleet of B-24s, which found their way using maps supplied by the OSS, would also fly armaments and explosives from England directly into Stockholm's Bromma Airport. From there, it would be taken by truck to an apartment-house cellar and stored until another truck arrived to smuggle the bounty over back roads into Norway—with guns concealed in hollowed-out logs under piles of timber.

Over time, thanks in large part to the OSS-coordinated work of Balchen's airborne fleet, the leaders of the Norwegian resistance movement grew bolder. Many of them, including Jens Christian Hauge, who worked for the OSS and was later a Norwegian government minister, traveled back and forth by rail between Oslo and Stockholm right under the nose of the gestapo.

Balchen's pilots and crews were also becoming bolder and more effective. "Before the war [was] over," he wrote, "we [were] supplying the reception committees with dynamite and TNT, winter underwear, sectional houses, fishhooks, even bales of hay for their horses."

One supply trip involved delivering fuel pumps to Malmö, in southern Sweden, to be used for refueling torpedo boats operated by US Navy Cmdr. Raymond R. Guest, head of the navy section at OSS headquarters in London, who was planning to run sabotage equipment from Sweden into Nazi-occupied Denmark.

Balchen was also instrumental in establishing an American air base at Kallax airport, near Luleå, in extreme northeast Sweden, which could be used to ferry supplies into northern Norway as the German forces were withdrawing to the west.

On 29 December, for example, Capt. Charles G. Hollyman, flying in clear weather with Balchen as copilot, led ten C-47s in two formations from Västerås to Kallax, escorted by Swedish fighter aircraft. On board was an entire Norwegian battalion whose men had been trained in Sweden, along with a complete field hospital with twenty-eight doctors, fourteen nurses, heating stoves, and a host of medical specialists.

On 7 January 1945, an attempt was made to transport thirty-seven Norwegians and nineteen tons of equipment into northeastern Norway at Kirkenes. But the planes were forced to return to Kallax due to bad weather. A second attempt on 12 January, however, was successful and marked the first time that an Allied unit had landed in occupied Norway.

Over the next six months or so—until Balchen's mission in northern Norway ended in August 1945—his C-47 aircraft would transport 1,442 soldiers and about 1,100 tons of equipment from Kallax to Kirkenes, along with additional tonnage to Kautokeino, Bank, and Bodø as the Germans retreated west and south down along the Norwegian coast.

Deeply impressed by Balchen's achievements, OSS Chief William J. Donovan sent a letter of commendation to the Norwegian-born aviator and his men on 2 July 1945, expressing the OSS's "sincere appreciation of the outstanding cooperation you have given."

"Your supply drops have been one of the outstanding operations of the war, and you have transmitted intelligence of inestimable value to the Supreme Commander, Allied Expeditionary Forces," Donovan wrote. "This headquarters is fully cognizant of the fact that the operations . . . have been both difficult and hazardous, and, on many occasions above and beyond the call of duty. . . . You have carried out a task which at no time has had a precedent in the annals of American air history."[10]

In the meantime, the US Army Air Forces also launched massive bombing raids against Nazi-occupied Norway, beginning in the summer of 1943, when its aircraft struck strategic targets, including a large U-boat base at Trondheim and several factories producing magnesium, aluminum, and nitrates at Herøya.

That fall, in an operation codenamed "Operation Leader," twenty American bombers from the aircraft carrier USS *Ranger* also conducted a raid against German ships in the vicinity of Bodø, Norway, destroying five ships and damaging another seven. Two German aircraft were shot down in the ensuing air battle, and three American airplanes were destroyed and another crashed while landing.

Two Norwegian airmen accompanied the US attack force, providing advice on the local geography. It is believed that the operation seriously disrupted the German war effort by compromising the convoy system in the region and reducing shipments of iron ore. Several American airmen were killed in the operation.

At a ceremony on 4 October 1987 commemorating the operation, a Norwegian citizen, Gunnar Bernstein, said that "those of us . . . who witnessed the battle . . . looked upon the presence of the American aircraft as a reaching out of hands from brothers—a gesture, which in itself bore promise of a new dawn, a new future for our beloved Norway."[11]

As the war in Europe drew to a close, the OSS and other US government entities continued to cooperate with the Norwegian resistance as it sought to prevent the occupying German troops from causing further damage and death.

Leading that effort in part was a twenty-five-year-old US Army major from Minnesota named William Colby, who earlier had parachuted into France as commander of Team BRUCE in support of French resistance forces on the ground.

With that mission now complete, Colby was recruited in early 1945 to command the OSS-directed Norwegian Special Operations (NORSO) Group, whose 100 or so members—nearly all Norwegian Americans—were being trained to parachute into northern Norway to sabotage a railway line being used to move roughly 150,000 troops to Germany after they had been pushed out of Finland.

One of the group's most important operations, codenamed Operation Rype, began on the night of 24 March when Colby—who would later become head of the CIA—joined his fellow saboteurs in one of eight B-24 Liberators being dispatched from RAF Harrington air base in England to an intended drop zone on a frozen lake in the wooded mountains north of Trondheim.

After flying up the Norwegian coast for several hours, however, only four of the airplanes succeeded in dropping their human and material cargo anywhere near the target, Lake Jaevsjo. One airplane dropped its paratroopers fifty miles inside Sweden. Three other planes were forced to return to England.

"I was in one of the successful four planes and landed easily on the frozen lake," Colby later recalled. "It was midnight. I saw a bonfire built on a bed of logs, burning through the ground mist. I walked toward it. A tall figure was waiting. I took my pistol in hand, just in case. The prearranged password was, 'Is the fishing good in this lake?' I said in my rudimentary Norwegian. The proper response was, 'Yes, particularly in the winter.'"

The next day, Colby and his colleagues, along with six Norwegian resistance fighters, set off on a 100-mile, six-day cross-country ski trek—each man carrying a fifty-pound pack and taking turns pulling small toboggans weighed down with sixty pounds of explosives.

"It was a brutal journey," Colby recalled, "often through blinding blizzards in zero temperatures and involving the climbing of ice-covered boulder-strewn mountains and crossing lakes and streams."

Arriving at the Northland Railway, the men immediately saw their target: the Grana Bridge. But the German defenses were too formidable to risk an attack, so they picked a smaller target, the bridge at Tangen.

"We arrived about dawn, set our charges and waited for a possible train, in hopes of repeating the sabotage operation that our Norwegian colleagues had pulled off nearby some months before," Colby wrote after the war.

But the wait for a train became too long for comfort, so they decided to blow up the bridge immediately, leaving behind their small American-flag shoulder patches to show that they had done the job and to protect the local population from possible German retaliation. After resting for a few days, Colby and his men were off again conducting another railway sabotage operation, this time near Trondheim.

In early May, the war in Europe came to an end. But the work of the Colby-led NORSO Group was not yet over. At Namsos, about one hundred miles north of Trondheim, the local population was not convinced and wanted some visible assurance that the war indeed had ended, and the NORSO Group was chosen for the job. Now numbering about thirty men, the group took the same railroad that they had earlier blown up, since repaired by Russian POWs.

Arriving in Namsos, the group encountered a few remaining German soldiers. "My orders, wisely, were that we should show ourselves in Namsos but under no circumstances give a German an order or attempt to arrest or disarm him," Colby wrote. "This was an order easy to follow, as I had not the slightest idea of what I could do if a German refused to obey me."

At the same time, however, Colby was responsible for demonstrating to the local population that the war was over. So he telephoned the German commander and announced that at 9 a.m. the next day he would visit the German naval ships "to inspect them."

"Taking three NORSO members, all former Norwegian merchant mariners, I climbed aboard each ship, despite the seller looks of the crewmen," Colby wrote. "And that put an end to all demonstrations; the message was clear to all that the war indeed was over."[12]

Gary G. Yerkey *is an American author and journalist. A graduate of Ripon College with a BA in philosophy, he later undertook postgraduate work at the American University of Beirut and spent more than a decade in Europe reporting for Time-Life, ABC News,* The Christian Science Monitor, *and other US news organizations. His most recent book, published last year, is entitled* When the Yanks Came to Sweden: How Thousands of American Airmen, Spies and Diplomats Changed a "Neutral" Nation in World War II. *He has also served in the US Air Force and is a former pilot. In 2015, he was among those who collectively received the Congressional Gold Medal for participating in the 1965 Selma to Montgomery voting rights march, led by Martin Luther King Jr.*

NOTES

1. US Department of State, Office of the Historian, *Foreign Relations of the United States Diplomatic Papers, 1940, vol. 1, General* (US Government Printing Office, 1959), document 58.
2. Florence Jaffray Harriman, *Mission to the North* (J. P. Lippincott, 1941), 251–54.
3. "U.S. Army Keeps Watch on War in Scandinavia," *New York Times,* 12 April 1940.
4. Harriman, *Mission to the North,* 257–89.
5. "Americans in Oslo Escape to Sweden," *New York Times,* 25 April 1940.
6. Harriman, *Mission to the North,* 287–88.
7. Marc Lancaster, "Robert Losey, the First U.S. Serviceman Killed in World War II," *World War II on Deadline* (Substack), 21 April 2021, https://ww2ondeadline.substack.com/p/robert-losey-first-american-killed-ww2.
8. Harriman, *Mission to the North,* 287–89.
9. Mrs. Loret Miller Ruppe, "Dombås Memorial Park, April 21, 1990," speech on the occasion of the 50th anniversary of the German Invasion of Norway, available at Barrington Area Library, https://balibrary.org/files/losey%20docs%2004.pdf.
10. Bernt Balchen, *Come North with Me* (E. P. Dutton, 1958), 215–98.
11. Bernstein quoted in personal letter, Captain Steve Millikin, "Regarding Norwegian Ceremony to Commemorate Operation Leader," 9 August 1993, US Navy Archives, Naval History and Heritage Command, Washington Navy Yard, Washington, DC.
12. William Colby, *Honorable Men: My Life in the CIA* (Simon & Schuster, 1978), 44–52.

Seven Generations

A CENTURY OF NORWEGIAN-AMERICAN HISTORY

J. R. Christianson

Dreams of Museums and Archives

Ole Edvart Rölvaag was a young fisherman in stormy Norwegian waters near the Arctic Circle in 1895, when Adolf Bredesen stood up at a meeting in Red Wing, Minnesota, to propose building a Norwegian-American museum. Norwegian-American institutions were not created, Bredesen said, by "some multi-millionaire in the East, some merchant prince, coal baron or oil king, but by the [hard]-handed Norwegian pioneer on the prairies and in the backwoods of Wisconsin, Iowa, and Minnesota."[1] It was time to acknowledge the Norwegian pioneers in America by building a museum and an archive that showed what they had achieved. Bredesen proposed that his alma mater, Luther College, should do this by collecting "relics and papers" that told the history of Norwegians in America. His proposal would eventually result in two enduring institutions:

the Vesterheim Norwegian-American Museum and the Norwegian-American Historical Association.[2]

Luther College immediately accepted Bredesen's proposal. Professor Haldor J. Hanson was put in charge, and in the years 1895–1902 he built a "folk museum" modeled after the Norsk Folkemuseum in Oslo.[3] It was far different from American museums. The Scandinavian folk museum presented the lives of ordinary people instead of displaying the fine art of renowned artists.[4] Hanson built the first one in America, and the Luther College library established an archive with the world's largest collection of Norwegian-American newspapers.[5]

Hanson left Luther College in 1902. A succession of other faculty curators took over leadership of the museum, and in the years 1911–1921, the college president, Christian Keyser Preus, served as curator. In 1913, Preus began to add an "open-air" collection of furnished buildings to present Norwegian-American pioneer life in a new way. The open-air museum also originated in Scandinavia with King Oscar's Collection in 1882, and the one in Decorah was the first in America.[6]

After President Preus's sudden death in 1921, Knut Gjerset took over as curator. Gjerset was born in Norway, grew up in America, studied at Minnesota, Johns Hopkins, and Heidelberg in Germany, and then went on to study in Oslo and Berlin. English, Norwegian, Danish, German, Latin, and Old Norse were no strangers to him. This erudite and cosmopolitan scholar took charge of the museum and began to plan for expansion.

Gjerset knew it would be a race. Others were also dreaming of a Norwegian-American museum. In 1912, thirty-four *bygdelags* representing immigrants from all parts of Norway began planning a centennial celebration of the Norwegian constitution on 17 May 1914 at the Minnesota State Fairgrounds in St. Paul. Their archives committee, led by President D. G. Ristad of Park Region Luther College in Fergus Falls, Minnesota, wanted to follow up the celebration by establishing a Norwegian archive and folk museum at the University of Minnesota, where the university's Scandinavian Department under Professor Gisle Bothne would serve as the foundation "for deeper research of the Norwegian element in the American nation."[7]

Two decades had passed since Bredesen's proposal, and O. E. Rölvaag was now a professor at St. Olaf College. He did not like the university plan and attacked it vigorously in the Norwegian-American press because he supported the museum at Luther College. He and Knut Gjerset were old friends. In 1920, Rölvaag tried without success to recruit Gjerset to become head of the Norwegian Department at St. Olaf College. Gjerset had acquired an international reputation as the author of a 1913 two-volume *History of the Norwegian People,* followed in 1924 by his *History of Iceland,* widely recognized as the finest histories of Norway and Iceland in the English language.[8] Rölvaag was well-known as a novelist and essayist in Norwegian but was not widely known to the English-speaking public.

In July of 1924, Norwegian-American newspapers throughout the land announced that the *bygdelags* behind the 1914 celebration at the Minnesota State Fairgrounds were now planning an even bigger "Norse-American Centennial" in 1925, celebrating the 1825 arrival in New York of the sloop *Restauration* from Stavanger with fifty-three Norwegian immigrants. Professor Gisle Bothne of the University of Minnesota was in charge of planning the celebration, and Twin Cities residents dominated all the central committees and subcommittees. There seemed to be some hope that this event would finally lead to the construction of the Scandinavian museum and center at the University of Minnesota.

Virtually no professors from Norwegian-American colleges were involved in the planning. Olaf Morgan Norlie from Luther had agreed to write the official history of Norwegians in America, and Rölvaag was asked to speak for fifteen minutes in Norwegian on "our ancestral heritage."[9] Bothne did not want college faculty members muscling in on the planning, although he did invite St. Olaf and Luther College students to participate as athletic teams and musical organizations.

Bothne knew that Dr. Anders Sandvig of Maihaugen museum in Lillehammer had proposed sending a collection of artifacts from Norwegian folk museums to America to remind the immigrants of "the homes they had left" and that Professor A. W. Brøgger of the University of Oslo was in charge of collecting many truckloads of museum objects.[10] Olaus Islandsmoen from the

Hadeland Folk Museum was traveling around America in search of the best place to deposit them.[11] This could be the answer to the dream of a Norwegian museum in Minneapolis.

The same 18 July 1924 issue of *Decorah-Posten* that announced the "Norse-American Centennial" included a suggestion by Carl L. Tellefsen, the paper's correspondent in Washington, DC, that 1925 would be a good time to establish a Norwegian-American historical society.[12] Kristian Prestgard's editorial in the same issue of *Decorah-Posten* endorsed Tellefsen's proposal. Prestgard drew on his own experience as an editor of *Symra,* the finest Norwegian literary and historical periodical published in America, and said that the best way to start a historical society would be to establish an archive to preserve, organize, and catalog Norwegian-American documents in both Norwegian and English.[13] The Luther College library already had a large collection of newspapers, letters, and other archival sources in a fireproof, state-of-the-art building and was collecting everything published in the Norwegian language in America. Prestgard thought that this archive should be transformed into a national institution. In due time, it would become the home of a historical society, and eventually the historical society could publish a journal. The last step would be to write the history of Norwegians in America.[14] Here in a nutshell was a plan that would be realized one year later in the Norwegian-American Historical Association, except that the location was transferred from Luther to St. Olaf.

Tellefsen's suggestion was widely discussed in the Norwegian-American press, but it was often connected with the plan for a museum in the Twin Cities.[15] In October of 1924, Bothne responded by putting the organization of a Norwegian-American historical society on the agenda of the 1925 Norse-American Centennial.[16] Rölvaag and Gjerset began to prepare for the worst.[17]

The Norse-American Centennial of 1925

Eventually, it proved impossible to organize that immense, four-day Norse-American Centennial without involving the colleges. Bothne and his committee wanted to fill the Minnesota State Fairgrounds with exhibits during the entire duration of the celebration, but neither the *bygdelags* nor the University of

Minnesota seemed able to put any exhibits together. The Minnesota Historical Society was willing to do only one exhibit. At the last moment, in January of 1925, Bothne's committee, in desperation, asked Gjerset to take charge of the exhibits. He seemed to be the only Norwegian American with museum experience.

Gjerset was growing old, and he had a weak heart. He was scheduled to teach a full load at Luther College, but his friend Prestgard helped him negotiate terms that gave him a free hand and generous budget, and he agreed to take on the immense task as an overload.[18] Once in charge, he dove right in. As early as 11 February 1925, he was able to inform Bothne that he had lined up a long list of St. Olaf and Luther professors to speak, write, or collect objects and make maps, charts, and graphs. Suddenly, the Twin Cities focus of the celebration was wedged wide open and the program was jammed full of lots of St. Olaf and Decorah people. Moreover, Gjerset told Bothne he didn't want any guides dressed in Norwegian folk costumes or a reenactment of a Norwegian peasant wedding, as some had suggested, because that would give "the American people the idea that we are a crude and primitive people without real culture." The implication was that a folk museum at the university, not far from the Minneapolis Institute of Art, would have the same negative effect. Gjerset's plan was for exhibits displaying Norwegian and Norwegian-American life at all levels of society with an overall emphasis on modernity and progress.[19]

Everything was ready when the great celebration of Norwegian-American ethnicity took place on 6–9 June 1925. The oversized political clout of Norwegian-American politicians, together with the Coolidge administration's emphasis on American "whiteness," transformed it into a national event attended by the president and First Lady, among a host of governors, senators, and congressmen of Norwegian birth or ancestry. Gjerset's twenty-two exhibits gave throngs of visitors a dazzling, new view of their own history and achievement as Norwegian Americans. "Ethnicity is not inherent," said historian April Schultz in retrospect, "but constructed as a dialogue between immigrants and the dominant society."[20] Immigrants and their descendants had been denigrated only a few years earlier as so-called hyphenated Americans of questionable loyalty, but now they began to take pride in being both Norwegian and American at the same time. Even those who didn't speak Norwegian could share in this pride. One woman said she couldn't see "any conflict at all in my two inheritances, the one from Norway the one from America. They fit together perfectly. I think I am richer for having the two instead of only the one."[21] The Norse-American Centennial of 1925 led to a major redefinition of what it meant to be Norwegian in America.

The time was ripe for new institutions that embodied this new sense of Norwegian-American ethnicity. Bothne had scheduled the meeting to form a Norse-American historical society for ten o'clock on Monday morning in the St. Louis County Building on the fairgrounds, but he was much too busy to attend because he was preparing to welcome President Coolidge and all those governors that same afternoon. The result was that the meeting never took place.[22] Gjerset and Prestgard were the only ones who showed up at ten. Young Theodore "Ted" Blegen, who had been on Gjerset's committee, and two others trickled in later.[23] Then, everybody simply left.

Gjerset's Dream

After the celebration, Gjerset kept thinking about that plan to establish a Norse-American historical society in Minneapolis. He knew all about the collection of artifacts coming from Maihaugen and other Norwegian folk museums.[24] In his opinion, they belonged in the Decorah museum, since that was the only Norwegian-style open-air folk museum in America. He talked it over with Prestgard, and they decided to act.

On 24 July 1925, Prestgard called a meeting on the front porch of his Decorah home, "Trollhaugen."[25] The aim was to find a "secure place" for the Decorah museum in any plan for a Norwegian-American historical society.[26] Gjerset proposed making the Luther College museum into a national Norwegian-American center that would include Prestgard's idea for a national Norwegian-American archive and historical society. He presented his plan for a "Society for the Preservation of Historical Relics and Records of Norse-American Pioneer and Cultural Life," which linked this center in Decorah to a future Scandinavian museum of fine arts—not folk arts—in the Twin Cities and an expanded library of Norwegian literature and music at St. Olaf College.[27] Gjerset's plan was discussed and finally endorsed after the St. Olaf part was omitted. Then, those in attendance chipped in funds to send Gjerset on the road in search of broader support.

Off he went the next day.

In the meantime, Prestgard printed up but did not circulate the final version of the plan and attached the names of fifteen "members," including a college president, a former governor, prominent church leaders, professors, and donors with deep pockets. When Gjerset returned from his travels through Minnesota to Madison and Chicago, he sent a copy of the printed statement to Rölvaag with a handwritten note in English on the back, highlighting the fact that the St. Olaf library was still part of the plan in his opinion.[28]

Rölvaag, however, was at his cabin in northern Minnesota, out of touch and deep into writing his next novel.[29] It took a while for the mail to arrive, and even longer for the two of them to get together. Gjerset wanted the two of them to meet with Prestgard and Ristad.[30] Unfortunately, Ristad could not be present when Prestgard and Gjerset finally came to Northfield to meet with Rölvaag and several others.

Separating the Archive and Museum

They came into a firestorm. Rölvaag and his Northfield friends didn't like the plan for a combined Norwegian-American museum, archives, and historical society in Decorah. St. Olaf College was already collecting Norwegian and Norwegian-American literature and setting its sights on becoming "the dominant center of Norwegian culture in America."[31] Many in Northfield saw Rölvaag's Decorah friends as competitors, not allies, and did not trust them as Rölvaag himself did. Those who were willing, however, sat down to work things out.

The details are unclear, but they must have zeroed in right away on the two central elements in Gjerset's proposal: the museum and the archive. Those two key elements were soon separated. Gjerset's primary concern, then and always, was the museum, which belonged to Luther College and couldn't be moved, but so did the vast collection of Norwegian-American newspapers, which Prestgard had envisioned as the foundation for a national Norwegian-American archive.

At one point, somebody must simply have asked something like, "What if the museum and the newspapers were to stay in Decorah and we decided to establish an entirely new Norwegian-American archive at St. Olaf College?" Prestgard's experience led him to think that a historical society and periodical would grow out of the archive. And what if that periodical were to be in English instead of Norwegian?

Eventually, Rölvaag, Gjerset, and Prestgard decided to travel together to the Twin Cities and on to Eau Claire, Wisconsin, to talk with the influential Norwegian-American editor Waldemar Ager, even though he, like Prestgard and Rölvaag, wrote mainly in Norwegian.[32] In the Twin Cities, they may have talked with young Theodore C. Blegen. He was American-born but fluent in Norwegian and had done a lot of translating and editing at the Minnesota Historical Society. Both Rölvaag and Gjerset knew him.

By the time Prestgard and Gjerset returned to Decorah, the group worked out the broad outlines for two related sister organizations, a Norwegian-American historical museum in Decorah and a Norwegian-American historical archive in Northfield. Prestgard wrote to Rölvaag on 30 September 1925 and said that they were ready to proceed, despite objections he had received from Bothne. "I have had two long and very strange letters from him," wrote Prestgard. "He is feeling the pain—more or less in general—but his argumentation is crazy."[33] The colleges and their allies had outflanked the university, and Bothne knew it.

Founding the Norwegian American-Historical Association

An organizational meeting for the Society for the Preservation of Historical Relics and Records of Norse-American Pioneer and Cultural Life was held in Northfield on 6 October 1925, just prior to the next convention of the Norwegian Lutheran Church in America in the Twin Cities. This allowed supporters from far and wide to attend on their way to the convention. Gjerset, Prestgard, Rölvaag, and Ristad met in Northfield on 5 October to finalize the agenda. Ristad had been won over to a museum in Decorah instead of Minneapolis.

These four natives of Norway had all lived in America for decades. Rölvaag was the youngest, but he was over fifty, and all of the others were more

Figure 1. The four founders of NAHA—Kristian Prestgard, O. E. Rölvaag, D. G. Ristad, and Knut Gjerset—with other members at the first meeting of NAHA's exective board after incorporation, 26 May 1926, Decorah, Iowa. Courtesy of the Luther College Archives, Decorah, Iowa.

than a decade older. Rölvaag and Gjerset both suffered from chronic heart disease. Gjerset was the powerhouse and the organizer with connections. Ristad later gave him credit for setting the whole project in motion and enlisting wide support not only in Decorah and Northfield but also in Madison, Chicago, and throughout the Midwest. Gjerset was also the one who wrote the draft constitution and bylaws presented at the meeting the following day, and he must have made many of the suggestions for a proposed slate of officers.

A large group attended the meeting in Northfield on 6 October 1925. After a long and thorough discussion, the assembled group voted to accept the revised plan embodied in Gjerset's draft constitution and bylaws, and they went on to elect officers.[34] A board of publications consisting of Gjerset and Prestgard was named to serve under Blegen as managing editor. All of Gjerset's far-flung contacts from the centennial were paying off.

Although the meeting had been called in the name of the Society for the Preservation of Historical Relics and Records of Norse-American Pioneer and

Cultural Life, that was not the name they chose for the new organization. Rölvaag had suggested "Symra," but that wasn't it either. It would be the Norwegian-American Historical Association (NAHA). These older men's memories were still of *heime* ("home") and *Norge,* but they looked to the future of their people in America and founded an association to preserve their Norwegian-American heritage in the English language.

The Norwegian-American Historical Museum

On 15 October 1925, the museum in Decorah was given the new name of the Norwegian-American Historical Museum by the board of trustees of Luther College on Gjerset's recommendation.[35]

Before long, Professor Brøgger contacted NAHA and asked where to send the gift of artifacts from Norwegian folk museums, including all the furnishings for a traditional Gudbrandsdal house from Sandvig's Maihaugen museum in

Figure 2. The Norwegian-American Historical Museum in 1936. Courtesy of Vesterheim Norwegian-American Museum, Decorah, Iowa.

Lillehammer. NAHA's board voted on 26 May 1926 to accept the gift and place it in the perpetual custody of the Norwegian-American Historical Museum.

Before long, five truckloads of artifacts arrived in Decorah. Gjerset jammed them into storage in the museum building on campus and set about to raise funds and find a bigger building. It took until 1932. A three-story brick building in downtown Decorah became available, and Gjerset, the weary and haggard old warrior who had written NAHA's first historical monograph by then and was working on another, finally began to build the finest museum of any ethnic group in America with the stalwart support of Rölvaag and many others.[36]

Rölvaag as NAHA Secretary

The Norwegian-American Historical Association was formally established at the first meeting of its executive board in the Ryan Hotel in St. Paul on 3 February 1926. Ristad became the first president of the board, Birger Osland of Chicago soon became treasurer, and Rölvaag agreed, reluctantly, to serve as NAHA's secretary, but only if his colleague J. Jørgen Thompson would agree to be his assistant, and so it was arranged. Thompson was a second-generation Norwegian American and St. Olaf graduate who had spent one year of study in Norway.[37]

Rölvaag dove into the task of organizing the NAHA office and soon established a model of leadership that endured for decades. It took a lot of time away from his writing but contributed to his goal of making St. Olaf a center of Norwegian culture in America. By the end of 1926, NAHA had nearly 800 members; one year later, it had a thousand. Rölvaag and Osland collaborated in the task of establishing an endowment, and before long, a research fund was also established in Norway by a wealthy British-Norwegian businessman, Sir Karl Knudsen.

Rölvaag and Thompson also began to organize a NAHA archive. It had to be done from the ground up because Luther College's collection of Norwegian-American newspapers and manuscripts remained in Decorah. St. Olaf College provided the space free of charge, and the two men began to solicit donations of books, manuscripts, correspondence, and anything else in writing that related to Norwegians in America. In retrospect, Kenneth Bjork later wrote, "Rölvaag's greatest single contribution to the association was perhaps his work in the archives."[38]

When Rölvaag died in 1931, Thompson carried on as NAHA's voluntary secretary and archivist while also serving as dean of men at St. Olaf College. He and Rölvaag had written hundreds of letters asking people to make donations to the archives. The time had come to go out and meet those prospective donors face-to-face.

Qualey and the Archives

In the summer of 1932, NAHA hired a Columbia University graduate student named Carlton C. Qualey, originally from Spring Grove, Minnesota, to visit Norwegian-American settlements in search of letters, diaries, farm and business records, newspapers, and other material that shed light on the lives of Norwegian immigrants and their descendants. Qualey hit the road in June and July and then spent part of August with a stenographer cataloging the pile of books, pamphlets, serial publications, newspapers, photographs, and manuscripts he had brought in, many of which are still in the NAHA archives. Qualey then composed rules and a guide for the use of the archive and recommended that it should be cataloged in detail by a professional archivist. He also recommended that NAHA should continue to send out field agents because the sources "do not readily come in of themselves."[39] This was not done.

Blegen and Thompson

NAHA's Articles of Incorporation laid out the association's five aims: (1) maintain and develop an archive, (2) support the Norwegian-American Historical Museum, (3) encourage Norwegian-American historical research and literary production, (4) publish monographs, and (5) publish a periodical "devoted to Norwegian-American history, literature, and culture."[40]

The description of a periodical devoted to "history, literature, and culture" sounded a lot like the old *Symra* edited by Prestgard and others, or else the *American-Scandinavian Review* edited by Hanna Astrup Larsen, but that was not what Blegen had in mind. He had studied under eminent American historians, Wallace Notestein and Solon J. Buck, and he intended to follow in their footsteps. In the 1920s, this meant starting with the famous "frontier thesis"

Figure 3. Editor Theodore C. Blegen in 1960. Courtesy of the Norwegian-American Historical Association, Northfield, Minnesota.

of Frederick Jackson Turner (1861–1932), which asserted that American civilization was born on the frontier as it moved westward across the continent. "In the crucible of the frontier the immigrants were Americanized, liberated, and fused into a mixed race, English in neither nationality nor characteristics," said Turner.[41] Blegen wanted to show that Norwegians were a part of this process. He left out Leif Erikson and the Vikings but otherwise adapted the story told by earlier chroniclers like Svein Nilsson and Rasmus B. Anderson and followed their trail of Norwegian pioneers from the Sloopers settling in upstate New York to others on the Midwestern and Texan frontiers. Blegen was a professional historian like Gjerset, and he stripped the Norwegian-American story of all filiopietistic exaggerations as he recast it into critical, objective history, complete with footnotes, bibliography, and illustrations. He was just getting started when Rölvaag's *Giants in the Earth* became a bestseller in 1927 and showed how Norwegian frontiersmen interacted with Santee Dakota and Irish, Danish, and Yankee settlers, as well as Norwegians from other parts of Norway. Blegen took a different approach. He disregarded Rölvaag's and Turner's emphasis on the multicultural nature of the American frontier.[42] Instead, he focused on the inner life of scattered Norwegian communities in America and also went back across the ocean to explore the old-world background more deeply than Turner had ever done.

Another innovative part of Blegen's approach was his emphasis on letters, diaries, guidebooks, songs, and other documents produced by the immigrants themselves. This was what he called "grass roots history."[43] When a Guggenheim Fellowship allowed him to study in Norway in 1928, he discovered and gave letters from immigrants the name of "America letters," using them to show how the immigrants spoke for themselves and built their own grass-roots transatlantic sense of community. He published America letters and other Norwegian sources in English translation in what he called NAHA's "Travel and Description Series."

During his thirty-five years as NAHA's editor, Blegen edited eight volumes of immigrant letters, dairies, and guidebooks, including *Frontier Mother: The Letters of Gro Svendsen,* a book he loved, and one of NAHA's all-time bestsellers, *The Diary of Elisabeth Koren, 1853–1855.*[44] He was unusually open, for the time, to women as authors and as the subjects of history. All in all, forty-one books were published by NAHA during Blegen's years as editor, including twenty volumes of *Norwegian-American Studies* brimming with articles and translations on all kinds of Norwegian-American subjects.[45] His monumental two-volume survey of the first century of Norwegian communities in America, *Norwegian Migration to America, 1825–1860* (1930) and *Norwegian Migration to America: The American Transition* (1940), summed up the entire story in vivid detail.[46] Blegen's focus as an author and editor was always on the frontier; he wanted to show how Norwegians established American communities of their own and helped to build the nation from the ground up. The destruction of Native American communities by violence and colonization was not a part of the historiography of his era. Memoirs by Osland and Laurence M. Larson, Karen Larsen's biography of President Laur. Larsen of Luther College, and a memoir of prairie life by Aagot Raaen offered personal glimpses into Norwegian-American life. Qualey contributed a meticulous study of Norwegian settlement prior to 1900, and Arlow William Andersen explored the early Norwegian view of American politics.[47]

Through all these years, Thompson carried on as NAHA's secretary and archivist in the manner established under Rölvaag, even while serving as acting president of St. Olaf College in 1942–1943. He was assisted in the years 1944–1959 by Josephine Opsal. Eventually, he also enlisted Lloyd Hustvedt of the Norwegian Department to handle membership and edit the newsletter. When Thompson retired in 1958, the meticulous and quick-witted Hustvedt was ready to carry on as his successor, assisted at first by Charlotte Hughes.[48] All these secretaries and archivists, like the editors, served without pay, and they did everything they could to promote NAHA and help to make St. Olaf College a center of Norwegian culture in America. Hustvedt also recruited Leonora Hallan to assist with cataloging, and by 1960, she had cataloged some 5,000 books in the NAHA archives.

Blegen's retirement from NAHA and the University of Minnesota in 1960 was celebrated with a festive banquet featuring an address by Qualey, as well as a conference on immigration and American history involving stellar international scholars like Henry Steele Commager, Oscar Handlin, and Ingrid Semmingsen.[49]

This present writer was a graduate assistant in history in his twenties when he met Blegen in 1957. Blegen was dean of the graduate school at Minnesota and invited the history faculty to a lawn party at his home in University Grove.[50] I was a teaching assistant studying European history, not yet a member of NAHA, and did not know that Blegen and I traced our ancestry to the same parish in Norway.[51] My memory is of a charming, distinguished man with sparkling blue eyes who was willing to chat cordially at some length with a young graduate student. Since then, I have come to know every one of his successors in NAHA's first century.

Bjork and Hustvedt

The person appointed to succeed Blegen was not Qualey of Carleton College but Kenneth O. Bjork, professor of history at St. Olaf College. Bjork was not present at Blegen's retirement event because he was in Norway, concluding a year of research on a Fulbright scholarship. However, Bjork was not unknown to NAHA. A third-generation son of prosperous Norwegian-American merchants, he had grown up speaking a refined urban dialect of Norwegian and went on to earn a doctoral degree in European diplomatic history. Soft-spoken, decisive, and far-sighted, Bjork joined the St. Olaf faculty in 1937 and soon became a member of NAHA's editorial board.[52]

During Blegen's editorship, Bjork had published two remarkable volumes that broke free from the frontier and presented a more diverse and urban view of Norwegian-American life. Bjork's books stand alongside Blegen's big two as major interpretations of the Norwegian experience in America. His first was *Saga in Steel and Concrete* in 1947, which showed how Norwegian engineers and industrialists helped to shape the structure of urban America and how one of them even enriched life on Minnesota's lakes by inventing the outboard motor.[53] Bjork's second book, *West of the Great Divide* in 1958, revealed the variety of Norwegian lives in a western world of cities, ships and railroads, gold mines, and ocean fisheries more diverse by far than the farms and Norwegian settlements of the Midwest.[54] Clearly, NAHA was in for a new ride under its second editor.

At the same time, there was a lot of continuity in new collections of letters and journals by women and men on the frontier, biographies of prominent individuals like Blegen, and eight issues of *Norwegian-American Studies* filled with contributions by authors who were often Norwegian Americans themselves.

Bjork launched a Topical Studies series of books that challenged traditional views of the past. Jon Wefald's *A Voice of Protest: Norwegians in American Politics, 1890–1917* was the first one in 1971 and asserted that Norwegian politicians have generally been left of center in American politics, which was challenged by several later books. Lovoll's *Cultural Pluralism Versus Assimilation: The Views of Waldemar Ager* in 1977 focused on an issue of perennial

Figure 4. Kenneth O. Bjork, Odd Sverre Lovoll, and Lloyd Hustvedt, circa 1980. Courtesy of the Norwegian-American Historical Association, Northfield, Minnesota.

debate. Carl H. Chrislock's *Ethnicity Challenged: The Upper Midwest Norwegian-American Experience in World War I* in 1981 took on the anti-immigrant attitudes of a difficult period.

Bjork also started an Authors Series, with scholarly, well-written studies of Hjalmar Hjorth Boyesen, Rasmus B. Anderson, and Kristofer Janson, showing how immigrant authors became a part of American literary culture.

In 1960, at the beginning of Bjork's twenty-one years as editor, NAHA's energetic new secretary, Hustvedt, was determined to do something about the archives, which had languished under Thompson. He managed to persuade the president of St. Olaf to foot the bill for an experienced researcher, Beulah Folkedahl, who finally began cataloging manuscripts in the NAHA archives.[55] As she did so, she began to publish a regular feature, "From the Archives," in

Norwegian-American Studies, full of fascinating tidbits that enticed curious researchers to visit the archives and dig deep into its documents. She kept at it until her death in 1971, when Elaine Kringen came on board and soon became Hustvedt's assistant in every aspect of NAHA administration.

Beginning in 1964, Marion John Nelson and Lila Nelson took over leadership of the Norwegian-American Historical Museum. They added "Vesterheim" to the museum's name and recharged it with new energy. Folk art classes transformed visiting a museum from passive viewing into an active process of crafting objects inspired by the museum's collections. Costumed guides and demonstrators brought the open-air division alive, and Nelson helped to organize an annual Nordic Fest in Decorah. As Vesterheim modernized and expanded, students were eager to participate through a museum studies program at Luther College started by this author.

In those same years, Bygdelagenes Fellesraad, the council of *bygdelags,* got in touch with Bjork. They were looking for a scholar to write their history. At that time, Lovoll, a native of Norway with a transoceanic childhood and education, was living in North Dakota and looking for a dissertation topic. The combination clicked, and the Lovoll family moved to Minneapolis, where he dove into a dissertation on the *bygdelag* movement at the University of Minnesota under the distinguished immigration historian Rudolph J. Vecoli.[56] Lovoll mastered the approaches of the new social history and wrote his dissertation. In 1971, he joined the faculty of St. Olaf College.

One year later, NAHA's secretary commented on America's "Ethnic Renaissance" and said, "Being different is no longer a fault, but a virtue." Publishers were reprinting NAHA's early books, colleges were teaching immigration history and ethnic studies, and Vesterheim's new vigor was attracting attention. "Moreover," he said, "because of its early entry (1925) into ethnic studies, the NAHA will now perhaps more than before serve as a model for groups who are just getting their studies underway."[57] Lovoll was on top of all the latest trends, and so were others like Qualey. When a large group of new social historians who were involved in research on many racial and ethnic groups established the

Immigration and Ethnic History Society (IEHS), they turned to Qualey to edit their influential IEHS newsletter for many years.[58]

Lovoll thought that NAHA also needed to move into this new social history. "Times they were a-changin'," and if NAHA wanted to keep up, it needed more money to do so. The officers and board members still served as unpaid volunteers, and the total balance in all of NAHA's endowments and current funds was less than $60,000. At the triennial meeting held in the Minneapolis Athletic Club on 20 May 1972, Dr. Richard Giere and several others asserted a need for higher levels of fundraising. President Gunnar Gundersen promised to match donations to launch a new fund, while G. Norman Wigeland followed up with a gift of $2,500 and Arthur O. Davidson, an incoming board member, made his presence felt by pledging to match $1,000 in contributions to a forthcoming publication.

ScanPresence

Despite the optimism of these events, there were disturbing trends as well. The 1970 census revealed that immigration from Norway and other Scandinavian nations had fallen to a trickle and that first- and second-generation Americans from all five Scandinavian nations—Denmark, Finland, Norway, Sweden, and Iceland—made up less than 1 percent of the total US population. Even including all succeeding generations, people of Scandinavian descent were less than 5 percent of America. Ties of kinship with Scandinavia had become more distant, and Scandinavian-American attitudes had become different from those of the home countries, although many developments in contemporary Scandinavia were attractive to younger Americans.[59] Where was all of this heading?

To examine that question, a large conference called ScanPresence: The Scandinavian Presence in North America was convened at the University of Minnesota in 1973. Lovoll reported on the *bygdelag* movement and concluded that it was dying.[60] Qualey's deft, laudatory descriptions of NAHA and Vesterheim saw them as small, thriving institutions that would continue to thrive on the quality of their work, even as ethnic identity gradually became "a fringe thing."[61]

Einar Haugen summarized the entire conference by noting that ethnic awareness had persisted only in a "pitiful percentage" of Scandinavians in America and that many ethnic organizations "built on shallow soil," with only a few members who could "prepare an interesting program on a Scandinavian topic," but he noted that genealogical interest, travel, reading, and study were awakening what he called "secondary ethnicity" in some, even though Scandinavia remained "culturally marginal" to most Americans.[62] Qualey and Haugen were both members of NAHA's board of publications.

NAHA at Fifty

In the NAHA office in those years, Hustvedt and his right hand Elaine Kringen continued to manage correspondence, membership, the archives, and everything else and kept the membership informed through regular newsletters. In 1974, Hustvedt persuaded Charlotte Jacobson, a recently retired St. Olaf librarian, to become NAHA's archivist. She had deep Norwegian-American roots in the Decorah area and exceptional organizing skills for dealing with a steadily growing archive.[63] Around this same time, St. Olaf College received the first installment of a large five-year monetary gift to endow a King Olav V Professorship in Norwegian Studies, which was held by Hustvedt from 1978 until his retirement from teaching in 1987.[64]

NAHA's fiftieth anniversary celebration in 1975 heard Vecoli, director of the Immigration History Research Center at the University of Minnesota, praise NAHA as an "outstanding group of scholars who raised immigration history to a new literary and scholarly level."[65] On earlier occasions, scholars like Franklin D. Scott of Northwestern University in 1950 and Walter Muir Whitehill of Harvard and the Boston Athenaeum in 1963 had also spoken well of NAHA. Two books were published in the fiftieth anniversary year: Lovoll's solid *A Folk Epic: The "Bygdelag" in America* and a slender history of NAHA by Lovoll and Bjork, which ended with Bjork's long list of proposals for future publications.[66]

By 1979, after two decades of processing and cataloging by Beulah Folkedahl and Charlotte Jacobson, the NAHA archives were in such good shape that Hustvedt was able to publish a 158-page *Guide to Manuscripts Collections of the Norwegian-American Historical Association*.[67] It became the last of twenty-three books edited by Bjork during two decades as NAHA's managing editor. No other American ethnic group had anything like the pile of books that NAHA had published under its first two editors—and there was much more to come.

Bjork had groomed Lovoll to be his successor, but many other schools were looking for talented young scholars in the booming field of ethnic and immigration history. How could NAHA retain this talented editor when they didn't even pay him? The board had been discussing this problem for a long time, but it was Bjork who finally acted decisively. He was supported by his friend and colleague Clarence A. Clausen, who had translated and edited many books and articles for NAHA. In September of 1979, the NAHA newsletter contained Bjork's dramatic, carefully reasoned proposal for a "Chair in Immigration Studies." The proposal assumed that future editors would be professional historians teaching at some college or university. It aimed to establish a "Chair Fund" to compensate the editor's institution for released time: "For example, if the editor's full teaching load is six courses per year but, by special arrangement, he teaches only five courses, the Fund would reimburse the college or university an amount equal to one-sixth of the editor's salary as a faculty member." The fundraising goal would be $100,000. Bjork and Clausen each pledged $5,000 in matching funds to launch the fund.

The clarity and sophistication of this proposal revealed the hand of Bjork as an experienced academic administrator, teacher, author, and editor. It was supported in the same issue of the newsletter by Hustvedt's editorial and a straightforward appeal by President Arthur O. Davidson to "provide our future editors with favorable working conditions."[68] The fund was established, began to grow, and came to be called the Kenneth O. Bjork Chair Fund.

Scandinavians

Following the ScanPresence conference of 1973, a second conference, ScanPresence II, took place in Minneapolis in 1977, where this writer reported on Scandinavian-American archives, including the NAHA archives, and laid out some guidelines for ethnic archives.[69]

In 1979, scholars from NAHA, the Swedish-American Historical Society, Danish American Heritage Society, and representative Finnish-American and Icelandic-American leaders were invited to meet in Decorah for the first SIMCON: Scandinavian Immigration Conference, organized by this writer. The aim was to foster scholarly collaboration through existing organizations. This was followed by a larger conference, SIMCON II in 1981, cosponsored by Luther College and Symra Literary Society.[70] These conferences put NAHA's publications into a broader context of ethnic and immigration studies, which continued to become ever more important in American life.[71]

An essential part of NAHA's wider impact in those years was the strong connection with Norway that grew out of Lovoll's transoceanic contacts, together with a growing interest in migration studies among Norwegian scholars, who established NAHA-Norge in 1981. NAHA-Norge has since held annual meetings, published fifteen books, and sponsored more than a dozen international conferences on emigration and Norwegian-American history and culture. A memorandum of agreement between NAHA and NAHA-Norge was signed in 2014, and NAHA-Norge grew into a separate organization affiliated with NAHA.[72]

Lovoll and Hustvedt

Lovoll knew how to connect with this wider scene. He was the first managing editor of NAHA who was born in Norway and educated on both sides of the Atlantic. His transoceanic background transformed NAHA into a more international organization than ever before at the very time when migration studies were also becoming more global. Lovoll's own books appeared in Norwegian as well as English editions. He came from a family of deep-sea fishermen in Norway and the Pacific Northwest, and the Washington part of his background also allowed him to pick up quickly on Bjork's interest in the West.

Lovoll's first volume as NAHA's third editor was a collection of essays in honor of Bjork, containing a fine biographical sketch of Bjork and a witty essay by NAHA's editorial assistant, Helen Thane Katz, on the inner workings of the editing process.[73] Lovoll then edited three more translations of works by

Norwegian-American pioneers and Chrislock's book on challenges to ethnic identity during World War I.

Volume 29 of *Norwegian-American Studies* in 1983 presented seven innovative microstudies of emigration from Norwegian communities ranging from coastal fishing villages to high mountain farming valleys. They were written by Norwegian scholars and showed how local differences in economies, populations, and climates created unique circumstances that caused emigrants to leave different parts of Norway at different times. Taken together, they gave a new understanding of the complex patterns underlying emigration. Lovoll's connections with Norwegian scholars made this volume possible.

Volume after volume appeared as NAHA's pace of publication ramped up under Lovoll's energetic leadership. His own history of the Norwegian-American people, *The Promise of America,* appeared in 1984 in a large format that allowed lots of photographs, maps, and illustrations.[74] It was published jointly by NAHA and the University of Minnesota Press and became tremendously popular, going through a sequence of updated editions and also appearing in a Norwegian edition.

After editing half a dozen more books by other authors, including some splendid biographies and a book on a Norwegian-American comic strip, Lovoll put out his own pioneering work of ethnic urban history, *A Century of Urban Life: The Norwegians in Chicago Before 1930.*

In 1984, Lovoll organized a conference on Scandinavians and other immigrants in urban America.[75] It was reminiscent of the ScanPresence and SIMCON conferences in its focus on Norwegians and other Scandinavians, and it featured a keynote speaker, John Higham, and a commentator, Kathleen Neils Conzen, who placed the Scandinavian urban experience in a broader historical context.

Funding for the archives got a tremendous boost in 1985 when a donor, Sanford K. Fosholt, established a new NAHA fund initially called the Fosholt Archives Fund. Fosholt said that he had been cleaning out piles of the old Norwegian books, documents, and letters in the house of a deceased uncle when he came to realize that such things should be preserved and decided to do something about it. He handed over a check for $50,000 to NAHA's archivist, Charlotte Jacobson, who continued to serve as archivist until her death in 1995.[76] This was the largest gift NAHA had ever received and was later augmented by a bequest of $60,000 from Odmund L. Hydle.[77]

In 1984, Elaine Kringen retired as NAHA's assistant secretary. Hustvedt noted that she "brought efficiency, precision and integrity to her position. We shall miss her."[78] His search for a successor led to Ruth Hanold Crane by 1986, and Hustvedt was finally able to breathe easier again.[79] "Over time," wrote Hustvedt, "the NAHA has become a major operation by way of record keeping," and he commented that Crane stepped right in to take charge of it. "Nothing pleases her more than prompt payment of dues, and she does not mind writing out receipts for gifts. In fact, she seems to enjoy it."[80] Ten years later, Crane was still on the job, and Hustvedt was still in awe of her energy and perception: "Since the day Ruth arrived she has done the work of two."[81]

In 1991, Forrest Brown retired as head librarian of St. Olaf and took over as NAHA's archivist. His strong interest in Norwegian-American genealogy led him to encourage research in the NAHA archives by a growing number of people with similar interests, who often contributed the results of their research to the archives.

By 1990, more than a decade had passed since fundraising had begun for the Kenneth O. Bjork Chair in Immigration Studies. Some withdrawals had been made to pay for Mary Hove's work as Lovoll's editorial assistant and other publishing expenses, but the fund had still grown to $165,000. St. Olaf's endowment for the King Olav V Professorship in Norwegian Studies was more than $400,000. The fact that NAHA's secretary and editor were both St. Olaf faculty members led Hustvedt to propose that the two funds be combined to establish a King Olav V Chair in Scandinavian-American Studies. The occupant would teach half-time at St. Olaf and work half-time as editor of NAHA's publications. The fine-tuning of workloads in Bjork's 1979 proposal was not a part of this proposal. For it to go into effect, NAHA had to jumpstart its fundraising and raise the same amount the college provided.[82] This was done, and Lovoll became the first holder of the new chair in 1992.

The King Olav V Chair became the first such chair at any American college or university. It was established with fanfare and a splendid conference that produced another innovative NAHA publication, *Nordics in America: The Future of Their Past*.[83] That same year, NAHA moved into a new home in the St. Olaf library, alongside other special collections like the Kierkegaard Library and college archives, and the NAHA office acquired its first computer.

Lovoll kept turning out a torrent of publications, and NAHA members frequently received two or even three books a year. Orm Øverland's *The Western Home: A Literary History of Norwegian America* (1996) covered the entire field of Norwegian-American literature with keen perception.[84] In 1998, Lovoll's own *The Promise Fulfilled: A Portrait of Norwegian Americans Today* charted new paths in migration studies by examining how ethnicity endures as each new generation redefines what it means to be Norwegian.[85] No other study of the persistence of ethnic identity over many generations had ever been published.

More fine biographies, works on art and artists, several studies of religious leaders, and a second urban study of Norwegians in Brooklyn by David C. Mauk characterized the remainder of Lovoll's dazzling career as NAHA's managing editor. Even after his retirement in 2000, he continued to teach part-time at the University of Oslo and write books that opened new perspectives on Norwegian-American history.

The Norwegian American Historical Association celebrated the seventy-fifth anniversary of Norwegian immigration in 2000 by cosponsoring a conference with the Minnesota Historical Society entitled *Vandringer*: Norwegians in the American Mosaic, 1825–2000, chaired by the present author, who had been a member of the NAHA board since 1972. Equal numbers of Norwegian and American scholars presented insights into many areas, including Norwegian-American food, household furnishings, architecture, and family; Norwegian and Native American interaction; emigration of Sámi and Kven minorities from Norway to America; immigration and multiculturalism in contemporary Norway; and the life and works of authors like Thorstein Veblen and Robert Bly. The celebration included an exhibit titled *Painting by Minnesotans of Norwegian Background, 1870–1970* at the historical society's James J. Hill House and another titled *Norwegian-American Painting in Minnesota Today* at the Groveland Gallery, both curated by Marion John Nelson.[86]

NAHA celebrated its own seventy-fifth anniversary that same year with a banquet in Northfield and the release of a restored silent film from the 1925 Norse-American Centennial in St. Paul, as well as a special exhibit of ten paintings on loan from Vesterheim, which was now fully independent from Luther College.[87] Todd Nichol, a member of NAHA's board of directors and board of publications, organized a conference at Luther Seminary in St. Paul to explore many aspects of Norwegian-American religiosity.[88]

Going Professional

In 1999, Hustvedt stepped down after forty years as executive secretary of the Norwegian-American Historical Association. His monumental contribution to NAHA was made with wit, clear vision, and a firm hand, serving as the unpaid administrator of NAHA's archives, membership, newsletter, funds, and secretarial affairs for all those years. Hustvedt shared Rölvaag's goal of "making St. Olaf [College] the dominant center of Norwegian culture in America," and he tended to see his work for NAHA through the lens of this aspiration. In his day, Rölvaag had also been strongly dedicated to collaboration with NAHA's sister organization, the Norwegian-American Historical Museum, but this was not part of Hustvedt's vision.[89]

When Hustvedt retired, NAHA's board of directors realized that the days of depending on a voluntary executive secretary were over. Hustvedt's role gave way to the salaried position of administrative director held by Kimberly Holland, a lawyer and St. Olaf graduate, beginning in 1999. The transition away from seventy-five years of volunteer leadership inevitably affected NAHA's bottom line. A generous flow of bequests and donations had supported a vigorous publishing program unmatched by any other American ethnic organization, and NAHA's overall financial health was strong, but the problem was that most of its funds were restricted to specific uses. The Fosholt-Hydle Fund, for example, could only be used to support the archives. In NAHA's entire portfolio, only part of the Rölvaag Fund could be used to meet the soaring cost of a salaried administrative director plus NAHA's share of the King Olav V Professorship. A 2003 challenge grant of $100,000 by board member O. Jay Tomson helped to meet administrative costs and pay for a growing online presence, but NAHA's overall financial situation remained problematic.

Brown continued to serve as NAHA's unpaid archivist until the end of 2004 and launched a docent program of volunteers to guide family historians working in the archives. When he retired, Gary De Krey and Jeff Sauve, two St. Olaf faculty members, were engaged to provide part-time archival services for NAHA while docents continued to assist users and NAHA began to charge an archival user fee. In 2006, De Krey was upgraded to be NAHA's part-time archivist and Sauve became the assistant archivist for both NAHA and St. Olaf College.[90] This meant that NAHA took on additional expenses for paid archival staff.

Nichol and Renewal

Lovoll retired at the end of 2000, and Mary Hove, his editorial assistant for twenty years, also stepped down. Ruth Hanold Crane had retired in May as NAHA's assistant secretary. Todd W. Nichol of Luther Seminary was appointed Lovoll's successor in the King Olav V Chair. He was a church historian and NAHA board member whose previous publications revealed keen historical understanding of the history of Norwegian-American Lutheranism.[91]

Nichol's appointment was announced jointly by the presidents of NAHA and St. Olaf College. In the fall of 2000, he started teaching part-time at both St. Olaf and Luther Seminary while editing NAHA's publications, beginning with a 2002 volume honoring Lovoll with essays on the Norwegian-American experience in a multicultural context by European and American scholars.[92] Then came two books by European authors in 2004 and 2006 and Lovoll's study of Norwegian-American small towns, *Norwegians on the Prairie,* which won the prestigious Caroline Bancroft History Prize as the best 2006 American book on the westward movement. In 2007, NAHA and the University of Washington Press jointly issued Terje Leiren's translations of plays by Marcus Thrane.[93]

Christopher Thomforde became an enthusiastic supporter of NAHA and a member of the board while serving as president of St. Olaf College in the years 2001–2006. He and others proposed a closer relationship with the college as a way to help NAHA deal with soaring administrative expenses. President John R. Tunheim took up this proposal, and in the summer of 2005, the NAHA board began to review the association's mission and financial challenges and consider alternative organizational structures. That fall, six standing committees for governance, archives, publications, finance and budget, membership, and development became a part of the board's modernized structure, and negotiations continued with the college. The board was keenly aware of NAHA's fiduciary obligations as a Minnesota nonprofit organization, as well as its unique obligation to preserve and articulate Norwegian heritage in America. In addition, the importance of NAHA's ties to modern Norway was emphasized when Crown Prince Haakon of Norway visited the archives on 20 October 2005.

In the end, NAHA chose to remain an independent, membership-based nonprofit organization in long-term partnership with St. Olaf College. The presidents of the two organizations signed a collaboration agreement on 8 June 2006. St. Olaf gained the right to appoint two members of the NAHA board and assumed human resources responsibility for NAHA employees, while NAHA agreed to reimburse the college for costs. NAHA retained ownership of its archives and library but transferred the Fosholt-Hyde Fund to the college in return for St. Olaf providing space for NAHA's archives, library, and publications program. NAHA's Bjork and Publications Funds, which supported the King Olav V Chair, were transferred to the college, and in return, St. Olaf assumed financial responsibility for supporting the chair. NAHA pledged to continue raising funds to support its publications, archives, and library. St. Olaf's director of the Center for College History was recognized as NAHA's archivist, and the holder of the King Olav V Chair of Scandinavian-American Studies continued to serve as editor of NAHA's publications.

Implementation of the agreement went smoothly for two years, until the Great Recession of 2008 devastated NAHA's endowments and those of most other nonprofit organizations. NAHA did not publish a single book in the next three years, although several were in the works. Moreover, Holland and her family moved away in 2008, and she resigned at the end of that year. NAHA was left without an administrative director and without the funds to hire a new one.

These were tough times, but NAHA was a tough organization. Ever since 1925, volunteers, donors, and staff members had always been there because they believed in NAHA's mission, and now, volunteers picked up again and carried on. NAHA had sloughed its way through the Great Depression of the 1930s and World War II and knew that it could not stand still in the face of the 2008 recession. St. Olaf was not prepared to take on any costs beyond those specified in the collaboration agreement of 2006, so NAHA's volunteer leaders pitched in, carried on, and figured out how to remain independent and cover operating costs.

By 2009, President Tunheim could report that "the financial crisis that has affected everyone has made NAHA, like all non-profit organizations, more careful and cautious." The board was continuing to explore "different organizational models" while keeping the focus on NAHA's primary aims, which were to "have a strong publications program" and a growing, well-managed "archives accessible to all."[94] By the spring of 2010, after working its way through periods of financial uncertainty, avoiding financial crisis at every point, going twenty months without an administrative director, and steadily moving toward a solid financial future while keeping a clear focus on preserving the vision of NAHA's founders, President Tunheim announced:

> On March 6, [2010,] The NAHA Board met and decided that the timing was not right for a closer tie to St. Olaf. Our discussions with the College have been put on hold for now, with mutual good feelings. Instead, the Board voted to maintain NAHA's current structure and focus on bolstering the administrative staff and strengthening the organization's financial resources. Fortunately, NAHA's current financial status is solid. The Endowment has come back considerably after losses due to the stock market

> decline. Further, NAHA does not have a deficit and can move forward with its current resources. The Board is eager to augment its Endowment, however, and will concentrate on raising additional funds.[95]

NAHA was determined to remain independent and true to its mission. In 2010, Brian Rude took over as president and NAHA hired Jacqueline D. Henry, a St. Olaf graduate with an advanced degree in library and information science, in what she later described as her "dream job" as NAHA's administrative director. NAHA began to move forward with renewed optimism. The archive developed plans for expanded space with climate control to extend the life of fragile documents. Moreover, NAHA-Norge announced that it would meet for the first time in the United States in 2011 in order to participate in celebrating the sesquicentennial of Luther College, the oldest Norwegian-American college.[96]

King Harald V and Queen Sonja of Norway also participated in the celebration of Luther's sesquicentennial and went on to visit NAHA's office on 14 October 2011. NAHA's publishing program was back on track, and editor Nichol was able to present the king and queen with a copy of *Norwegian-American Studies* volume 36. In his address to a convocation at St. Olaf College, King Harald praised NAHA as the "voice" of the Norwegian-American community, "showing us the past" as it "also sheds light on our present" and helps to maintain the "strong connections" that "continue to bind America and Norway together."[97] This high praise from the King of Norway would inspire NAHA for years to come.

NAHA's fund balances remained positive through all of this increasing activity. Beginning in 2012, Øverland's monumental four-volume edition of America letters began to appear, one volume at a time in alternate years. In 2013, NAHA adopted a three-year strategic plan to strengthen its core functions of membership, archives, and publications.

When Henry retired in 2015, Amy Boxrud, senior writer at St. Olaf College and a NAHA board member, was hired as executive director and took charge of NAHA's fundraising, public relations, and membership programs. Members now met every other year instead of triennially, with tours and special events in between. The archives assisted ever-larger numbers of researchers as collections continued to grow. NAHA's invested fund balances were approaching $2 million.

Nichol retired at the end of the summer of 2017. The final volume of Øverland's book appeared in 2018, and so did Lovoll's memoir, *Two Homelands*. Both were edited and published by NAHA and distributed by the University of Minnesota Press and Minnesota Historical Society Press, respectively. De Krey retired as NAHA's archivist on the same day as Nichol, and Sauve shifted to working full-time for St. Olaf. With a new executive director in place and the prospect of a new editor and archivist, NAHA was ready for big changes.

Boxrud, Peterson, and Warner

With Nichol's retirement, the holder of the King Olav V Chair ceased to be the editor of NAHA's publications. The chair went to Margaret Hayford O'Leary, professor of Norwegian at St. Olaf, who held it until her death in 2018, and then to Dan Dressen, associate provost and professor of music, until 2021, when Kari Lie Dorer, professor of Norwegian at St. Olaf, was named the holder of the King Olaf V Chair of Scandinavian Studies.

In 2018, Anna M. Peterson, assistant professor of history and Nena Amundson Distinguished Professor at Luther College, became NAHA's fifth editor. She continued to teach history at Luther College, and NAHA returned to the original pattern of an editor who did not live in Northfield.[98] Peterson's immediate task was to redesign and relaunch *Norwegian-American Studies* as an annual publication in a new format. She accomplished this job with flair in 2019, transforming the journal into a well-illustrated journal of scholarship on the Norwegian-American experience and a forum for intellectual exchange on all aspects of Norwegian-American life, edited by NAHA and published annually in partnership with the journal program of the University of Minnesota Press.

Øverland's four volumes of Norwegian-American letters had been distributed by the University of Minnesota Press in the years 2012–2018, but Mauk's *The Heart of the Heartland: Norwegian American Community in the Twin Cities* and Bodil Stenseth's scandal-ridden tale, *Muus vs. Muus,* edited by Dorer, were copublished by NAHA and the Minnesota Historical Society Press. Lovoll's *Colonel Hans Christian Heg and the Norwegian American Experience* was published by the Minnesota Historical Society Press and distributed to NAHA members.

Kristell Benson became NAHA's part-time interim archivist when De Krey and Sauve left in 2017 until Kristina Warner took over as the NAHA archivist in March of 2019. When Covid-19 struck, it was difficult and at times impossible for researchers to visit the archives over the next two years. Warner moved rapidly ahead to update catalog records, create new finding aids, and digitize some at-risk materials. Two Minnesota Legacy Grants allowed the archives to take on the immense projects of digitizing the vast O. E. Rölvaag Collection, enlisting a full-time project imaging archivist and several student interns to assist with "scanning, describing, cataloging, and preservation of more than 23,000 digital files" and then taking on the equally immense Norse-American Centennial Collection.[99] These digital collections soon sparkled as never before and began to serve eager researchers around the world with crisp images of scanned photos and documents by the thousands.

Before and after Covid, Amy Boxrud organized NAHA's biennial meetings, trips to NAHA-Norge seminars in Norway, and all kinds of events for NAHA members. These included a tour of historic Norwegian-American churches in Minnesota and another of sculpture by Norwegian artist Jacob Fjelde in the Twin Cities. NAHA members also visited the North Shore of Lake Superior to learn about the history of commercial fishing by Scandinavian Americans to Minnesota. Nothing made the Norwegian-American experience more tangible than visits to landmark sites of Norwegian history in America.

By 2025, more young Americans were learning the Norwegian language and living for a time in Norway. Their generation challenged both NAHA and NAHA-Norge to draw them in and enlist their leadership to renew the focus and ranks of both organizations for generations to come. By that centennial year, the NAHA archives and St. Olaf's archives and special collections were in the process of moving into a newly renovated home in the Rolvaag Memorial Library, with a new archives vault and a reading room for researchers containing more than 950 *bygdebøker* and other genealogical resources. NAHA has never been

Figure 5. ***Left to right:*** **Executive director Amy Boxrud, archivist Kristina Warner, and editor Anna Peterson at the Norwegian Emigrant Museum near Hamar for the NAHA-Norge conference in 2022. Courtesy of the Norwegian-American Historical Association, Northfield, Minnesota.**

a genealogical society, but Dale Hovland, a volunteer trained by Brown, worked one-on-one with members and wrote several useful guides for genealogists as genealogical research became a way for many members to reconnect with their Norwegian roots.

NAHA prepared for its centennial with a new visual identity, a redesigned newsletter and website, and a new URL, norwegianamericanhistory.org. The public phase of "Archiving Norwegian America," a three-year centennial campaign to raise $2 million for an Archives Endowment Fund, was announced. Members celebrated the centennial year of 2025 by traveling to Sioux Falls, South Dakota, for the Pulitzer Prize–winning opera *Giants in the Earth* in the spring, attending NAHA's Crossings and Connections conference in Northfield in June, joining a NAHA-Vesterheim immigration tour of New York City in the fall, and celebrating together at a grand centennial banquet in Minneapolis on 25 October 2025.

Generations

What it means to be Norwegian American continues to change with every generation. In 1925, the immigrant founders of NAHA wanted to preserve a heritage their generation had brought from Norway for new generations who were born in America without memories of growing up in Norway. Many members of the second generation spoke Norwegian at home, but they lived in an English-speaking world and did not want to be seen as hyphenated Americans. Most of them did not teach their children to speak Norwegian. This meant that the third generation grew up "firmly rooted in American soil and accepted as an equal by his [or her] daily companions," as Marcus Lee Hansen wrote in 1938, but it also meant that the Norwegian language and much of their heritage was lost to them. When they came to realize what they had lost, they wanted to reconnect. As Hansen puts it, "What the son wishes to forget the grandson wishes to remember."[100] He was confident that this reconnection was possible because the "mental traits of creation and appreciation developed in any nationality through hundreds of years of community life are [not] lost in the course of one or two generations."[101] Hansen was the first to show that an ethnic identity has to be redefined by every new generation.

Sixty years later, Lovoll wanted to discover how the ethnic identity of Norwegian Americans had changed over a longer period of many generations. His 1998 book, *The Promise Fulfilled: A Portrait of Norwegian Americans Today,* revealed that many symbols of Norwegian-Americanness were "invented" by Norwegian Americans themselves and did not actually come from Norway. This produced an "eclectic confusion of earnest and silly ethnic expressions" including gigantic statues, symbolic trolls and nisser, Viking reenactments, Ole and Lena jokes, and symbolic foods from "a pure and simple ancestral homeland" that no longer existed.[102] Visitors from Norway found these lighthearted, invented traditions to be unlike anything in Norway.

However, Lovoll also discovered that there was more to being a Norwegian American than eating lutefisk and telling jokes. His interviews with 1,000 Norwegian Americans from coast to coast revealed a hidden ethnicity that often shaped their attitudes in ways they did not recognize as Norwegian. In the doctor's office, for example, Norwegian Americans turned out to need less anesthesia than the average American. They were not trying to be Norwegian in their tolerance for pain; it was just the way they were. They were also underrepresented in the very top echelons of the American economy. Lovoll discovered that this was because many Norwegian Americans "did not seek social advancement as an end in itself but instead preferred a congenial and cohesive community."[103] They preferred the happiness that came from living in a secure and trusting community over the pursuit of an American dream of great wealth and power. Norway always seems to rank toward the top in any international chart of honesty, social trust, and happiness, and the values of many Norwegian Americans turned out to be similar. Norwegian Americans were not opposed to success when it was achieved in what they considered to be an ethical manner. In fact, Lovoll found that upward mobility strengthened the ethnic identity of many successful Norwegian Americans he interviewed.

A quarter century later in the year 2025, the sixth and seventh generations of young Norwegian Americans continued to find new ways to identify with their ethnic roots. They studied Norwegian language and culture at the Concordia Language Villages, Luther College, St. Olaf College, and elsewhere, sometimes through online language courses. More of them were going to Norway, visiting, living, and studying there. They wanted to connect with the modern Norway of the Nobel Peace Prize, a strong commitment to outdoor activities, environmental values, and the resolution of conflicts around the world, a remarkably high level of happiness and security, and a commitment to using its national wealth for the good of its citizens and the world. These were values that spoke to new generations of Norwegian Americans and their friends.

The Norwegian-American Historical Association was here for them. NAHA is here for all generations, online and in print, wherever they are in the world. Its archives and publications contain an immense, growing database of information about the legacy of Norwegians in America, one that is unmatched by any similar organization in this wide, interconnected world of ours. Present and future generations will make this legacy their own.

***J. R. Christianson** taught European and immigration history at Luther College from 1967 to 1997 and established its museum studies program in cooperation with Vesterheim. He served as a member and officer of the NAHA board from 1972 to 2005. His current project is a book on Marcus Lee Hansen tentativly entitled* Why People Migrate.

NOTES

The author thanks two anonymous reviewers and others who read the manuscript, including Birgitte Christianson and Amy Boxrud, for their helpful comments.

1. David T. Nelson, "The Norwegian-American Museum," *Palimpsest* 46, no. 12 (1965): 613–14; A. E. Strand, ed., *A History of the Norwegians in Illinois* (John Anderson, 1905), 38.
2. [Historically, *Norwegian-American* has been hyphenated in NAHA's organizational name. Branding changes in 2024 led the organization to drop the hyphen in the name. For sake of consistency, the organizational name is hyphenated throughout this article.—Ed.]
3. "Haldor Johan Hanson," Luther College Library, 2 January 2025, https://www.luther.edu/library/about/collections/special.
4. Nelson, "Norwegian-American Museum," 615–20, 622–23.
5. Nelson, 615–20.
6. Nelson, 621–24.
7. N. N. Rønning, ed., *Syttende Mai Festskrift: Hundredeaars-Festen, Saint Paul-Minneapolis 1914* (K. C. Holter, 1914), 143; Odd Sverre Lovoll, *A Folk Epic: The "Bygdelag" in America* (Twayne Publishers for the Norwegian-American Historical Association, 1975); Lloyd Hustvedt, "The NAHA and Its Antecedents," in *Americana Norvegica,* ed. H. S. Naess and Sigmund Skard (Universitetsforlaget, 1971), 3:302. See also Gisle Bothne, "Nordiske studier ved amerikanske universiteter," in *Norsk-Amerikanernes Festskrift 1914,* ed. Johs. B. Wist (Symra, 1914), 334–37.
8. Knut Gjerset, *History of the Norwegian People,* 2 vols. (Macmillan, 1915); Knut Gjerset, *History of Iceland* (Macmillan, 1924). Gjerset was a Rankean scholar who strove to make history into fine literature. See Felix Gilbert, "What Ranke Meant," *American Scholar* 56, no. 3 (1987): 393–94.
9. "Indvandringsjubilæet," *Decorah-Posten,* 18 July 1924, 6. Professor Johan Andreas Holvik of Concordia College served on the executive committee.
10. Anders Sandvig, *I Arbeid og Fest* (John Grundt Tanum, 1947), 172–75.
11. David T. Nelson, "Knut Gjerset," *Norwegian-American Studies* (hereafter *NAS*) 25 (1972): 40.
12. "Fra Washington, D.C.," *Decorah-Posten,* 18 July 1924, 7.
13. Einar Haugen, "Symra: A Memoir," *NAS* 27 (1977): 101–10.
14. "Et norsk historisk Arkiv," *Decorah-Posten,* 18 July 1924, 4.
15. Odd S. Lovoll and Kenneth O. Bjork, *The Norwegian-American Historical Association 1925–1975* (Norwegian-American Historical Association, 1975), 15.
16. D. G. Ristad, "The Norwegian-American Historical Association," *NAS* 1 (1926): 149.
17. David T. Nelson, "Knut Gjerset," *NAS* 25 (1972): 36–37.
18. Gjerset to Bothne, 21 January 1925, file #1198, section I, Norwegian-American Historical Association Archives, Northfield, MN (hereafter NAHA Archives); S. H. Holstad to Gjerset, 26 January 1925, file #1198,section I, NAHA Archives; Prestgard to Bothne, 27 January 1925, file #1198, section I, NAHA Archives.
19. Gjerset to Bothne, 11 February 1925, file #1198, section I, NAHA Archives; *Norse-American Centennial Catalog of Exhibits Exclusive of Fine Arts,* file #1198, section III, NAHA Archives.
20. April Schultz, " 'The Pride of the Race Had Been Touched': The 1925 Norse-American Immigration Centennial and Ethnic Identity," *NAS* 33 (1992): 268–69; April Schultz, *Ethnicity on Parade: Inventing the Norwegian American Through Celebration* (University

of Massachusetts Press, 1994); David C. Mauk, *The Heart of the Heartland: Norwegian American Community in the Twin Cities* (Minnesota Historical Society Press and Norwegian-American Historical Association, 2022), 239–42.

21. Orabel Thortvedt in *Red River Girl / Jenta ved Red River*, ed. Tilman Hartenstein et al. (Vest-Telemark Museum and Historical and Cultural Society of Clay County, 2020), 167.
22. *Norse-American Centennial 1825–1925, Souvenir Edition* (Augsburg, 1925), 75.
23. Lovoll and Bjork, *Norwegian-American Historical Association*, 15; Hustvedt, "NAHA and Its Antecedents," 303.
24. Sandvig, *I Arbeid og Fest*, 172–75.
25. Kristian Prestgard, "From My Life as a Newspaperman in America," trans. Harry T. Cleven, *NAS* 35 (2000): 255.
26. Hustvedt, "NAHA and Its Antecedents," 303.
27. "Society for the Preservation of Historical Relics and Records of Norse-American Pioneer and Cultural Life," file #1198, section I, NAHA Archives.
28. Gjerset to Rölvaag, 10 August 1925, file #1198, section I, NAHA Archives.
29. The cabin has been moved to Sioux Falls, South Dakota. See Chuck Wood, "This Minnesota Home Is Literally at the 'Fork in the Road,' " Kickin' Country, 15 November 2021, https://kikn.com/this-minnesota-home-is-literally-at-the-fork-in-the-road/.
30. Prestgard to Rölvaag, 17 August 1925, NAHA Archives (my translation).
31. Kenneth Bjørk, "The Unknown Rølvaag: Secretary in the Norwegian-American Historical Association," *NAS* 11 (1940): 116.
32. Lovoll and Bjork, *Norwegian-American Historical Association*, 16.
33. Prestgard to Rölvaag, 30 September 1925, file #1198, section I, NAHA Archives: "Han er jo vond indvortes—saadan on general principles—men hans argumentation er sindssvag." On Bothne's later efforts on behalf of Norwegian-American celebrations in the Twin Cities, see Mauk, *Heart of the Heartland*, 263–67, 273.
34. Ristad, "Norwegian-American Historical Association," 149–50.
35. David T. Nelson, "Knut Gjerset," *NAS* 25 (1972): 41.
36. Knut Gjerset, "The Norwegian-American Historical Museum," *NAS* 6 (1931): 153–61; David T. Nelson, "The Norwegian-American Museum," *Palimpsest* 46, no. 12 (1965): 609–40.
37. *Norwegian-American Historical Association News Letter* (hereafter *Newsletter*) 7 (June 1958).
38. Bjørk, "Unknown Rølvaag," 141.
39. Carlton C. Qualey, "A Hunt for Norwegian-American Records," *NAS* 7 (1933): 95–120.
40. "Certificate of Incorporation of the Norwegian-American Historical Association," *NAS* 1 (1926): 152–55. The incorporators were Gjerset, Osland, and Rölvaag.
41. Frederick Jackson Turner, "The Significance of the Frontier in American History," in *Annual Report of the American Historical Association for the Year 1893* (Washington, DC: Government Printing Office, 1894), 216.
42. Several of Blegen's books with the University of Minnesota Press, including *Grass Roots History* (1947) and *The Land Lies Open* (1949), and his two histories of Minnesota have a multicultural focus.
43. Blegen, *Grass Roots History*.
44. Gro Svendsen, *Frontier Mother: The Letters of Gro Svendsen*, trans. and ed. Pauline Farseth and Theodore C. Blegen (Norwegian-American Historical Association, 1950);

Elisabeth Koren, *The Diary of Elisabeth Koren,* trans. and ed. David T. Nelson (Norwegian-American Historical Association, 1955).

45. Theodore C. Blegen, ed., *Studies and Records,* vol. 1 (Norwegian-American Historical Association, 1926); vol. 2 (1927); vol. 3 (1928); vol. 4 (1929); vol. 5 (1930); *Norwegian-American Studies and Records,* vol. 6 (1931); vol. 7 (1933); vol. 8 (1934); vol. 9 (1936); vol. 10 (1938); vol. 11 (1940); vol. 12 (1941); vol. 13 (1943); vol. 14 (1944); vol. 15 (1949); Kenneth Bjork, ed., *Norwegian-American Studies and Records,* vol. 16 (1950); Carlton C. Qualey, ed., *Norwegian-American Studies and Records,* vol. 17 (1952); Theodore C. Blegen, ed., *Norwegian-American Studies and Records,* vol. 18 (1954); Carlton C. Qualey, ed., *Norwegian-American Studies and Records,* vol. 19 (1956); Kenneth Bjork, ed., *Norwegian-American Studies and Records,* vol. 20 (1959).
46. Theodore C. Blegen, *Norwegian Migration to America 1825–1860* (Norwegian-American Historical Association, 1931); Theodore C. Blegen, *Norwegian Migration to America: The American Transition* (Norwegian-American Historical Association, 1940).
47. Carlton C. Qualey, *Norwegian Settlement in the United States* (Norwegian-American Historical Association, 1938); Arlow William Andersen, *The Immigrant Takes His Stand: The Norwegian-American Press and Public Affairs* (Norwegian-American Historical Association, 1953).
48. *Newsletter* (1958).
49. Henry Steele Commager, ed., *Immigration and American History: Essays in Honor of Theodore C. Blegen* (University of Minnesota Press, 1961); *Newsletter* (May 1960).
50. 1588 Northrop Street, Falcon Heights.
51. Olaf Morgan Norlie's parents also came from Fåberg near Lillehammer. Like old farming families in many Norwegian parishes, we were all three distantly related.
52. Odd S. Lovoll, "Kenneth O. Bjork: Teacher, Scholar, and Editor," in *Makers of an American Immigrant Legacy: Essays in Honor of Kenneth O. Bjork,* ed. Odd S. Lovoll (Norwegian-American Historical Association, 1980), 3–14; *Newsletter* (November 1960).
53. Kenneth Bjork, *Saga in Steel and Concrete: Norwegian Engineers in America* (Norwegian-American Historical Association, 1947).
54. Kenneth O. Bjork, *West of the Great Divide: Norwegian Migration to the Pacific Coast, 1847–1893* (Norwegian-American Historical Association, 1958).
55. *Newsletter* 10 (1960).
56. Odd S. Lovoll, *Two Homelands: A Historian Considers His Life and Work* (Norwegian-American Historical Association and Minnesota Historical Society, 2018), 147–54.
57. *Newsletter* 45 (March 1972).
58. Commager, *Immigration and American History,* 8–25, 96–106, 152. See also Carlton C. Qualey, "Immigration, Emigration, Migration," in *In the Trek of the Immigrants: Essays Presented to Carl Wittke,* ed. O. Fritiof Ander (Augustana College Library, 1964).
59. S. Ralph Cohen, "Avant Propos: The Statistical Background," in *The Scandinavian Presence in North America,* ed. Erik Friis (Harper's Magazine Press, 1976), 3–10.
60. Friis, *Scandinavian Presence,* 97–98. Genealogy has since revived it.
61. Carlton C. Qualey, "Norwegian-American Learned Societies," in Friis, *Scandinavian Presence,* 106–9.
62. Einar Haugen, "Summary Report of the Seminar," in Friis, *Scandinavian Presence,* 235–46.
63. *Newsletter* 76 (August 1988).

64. *Newsletter* 81 (December 1990).
65. Rudolph J. Vecoli, "An Outsider's View of the Association," *NAS* 27 (1977): 272–79; Franklin D. Scott, "Controlled Scholarship and Productive Nationalism," *NAS* 17 (1952): 130–58; Walter Muir Whitehill, "The Independent Historical Society," *NAS* 22 (1965): 198–209.
66. Lovoll and Bjork, *Norwegian-American Historical Association.*
67. Lloyd Hustvedt, ed., *Guide to Manuscript Collections of the Norwegian-American Historical Association* (Norwegian-American Historical Association, 1979).
68. *Newsletter* 58 (September 1979).
69. J. R. Christianson, "Scandinavian American Archives," *Bridge* 1, no. 6 (1981): 30–34, available at ScholarsArchive, Brigham Young University, https://scholarsarchive.byu.edu/cgi/viewcontent.cgi?article=2007&context=thebridge.
70. J. R. Christianson, ed., *Scandinavians in America: Literary Life* (Symra Literary Society, 1985), proceedings of SIMCON II.
71. H. Arnold Barton, "Where Have the Scandinavian-Americanists Been?," *Journal of American Ethnic History* 15, no. 1 (1995): 46–55.
72. "OM," NAHA-Norge Det norsk-amerikanske historielaget i Norge, accessed January 6, 2015, https://nahanorge.com/om/.
73. Lovoll, "Kenneth O. Bjork," 3–14, 210–15.
74. Odd S. Lovoll, *The Promise of America: A History of the Norwegian-American People* (University of Minnesota Press and Norwegian-American Historical Association, 1984).
75. Odd S. Lovoll, ed., *Scandinavians and Other Immigrants in Urban America: The Proceedings of a Research Conference, October 26–27, 1984* (St. Olaf College Press, 1985).
76. *Newsletter* 70 (July 1985); *Newsletter* 94 (April 1996).
77. *Newsletter* 104 (January 1999).
78. *Newsletter* 67 (April 1984).
79. *Newsletter* 72 (August 1986).
80. *Newsletter* 73 (February 1987).
81. *Newsletter* 94 (April 1996).
82. *Newsletter* 81 (December 1990); see also Hustvedt's editorial in the same issue.
83. Odd S. Lovoll, ed., *Nordics in America: The Future of Their Past* (Norwegian-American Historical Association, 1993).
84. Orm Øverland, *The Western Home: A Literary History of Norwegian America* (Norwegian-American Historical Association and University of Illinois Press, 1996).
85. Odd S. Lovoll, *The Promise Fulfilled: A Portrait of Norwegian Americans Today* (University of Minnesota Press, 1998).
86. Marion John Nelson, *Painting by Minnesotans of Norwegian Background 1870–1970* (Norwegian-American Historical Association, 2000).
87. *Newsletter* 110 (August 2000); *Newsletter* 112 (April 2001).
88. Todd W. Nichol, ed., *Crossings: Norwegian-American Lutheranism as a Transatlantic Tradition* (Norwegian-American Historical Association, 2003).
89. Bjork, "Unknown Rølvaag," 116.
90. *Newsletter* 124 (Spring 2005); *Newsletter* 128 (Spring 2006); *Newsletter* 131 (Spring 2007).
91. Todd Nichol, ed. and trans., *Vivacious Daughter: Seven Lectures on the Religious Situation Among Norwegians in America* (Norwegian-American Historical Association,

1990) deals with a clergyman in the Norwegian state church tradition. Todd Nichol, ed. and trans., "A Haugean Woman in America: The Autobiography of Sigrid Eielsen," *NAS* 35 (2000): 265–300, focuses on a woman in the Haugean tradition.

92. Todd W. Nichol, ed., *Interpreting the Promise of America: Essays in Honor of Odd Sverre Lovoll* (Norwegian-American Historical Association, 2002).
93. Jørn Brøndal, *Ethnic Leadership and Midwestern Politics: Scandinavian Americans and the Progressive Movement in Wisconsin, 1890–1914* (Norwegian-American Historical Association and University of Illinois Press, 2004); Johannes B. Wist, *The Rise of Jonas Olsen: A Norwegian Immigrant's Saga,* trans. Orm Øverland (University of Minnesota Press and Norwegian-American Historical Association, 2006); Odd S. Lovoll, *Norwegians on the Prairie: Ethnicity and the Development of the Country Town* (Minnesota Historical Society Press and Norwegian-American Historical Association, 2006); *Newsletter* 132 (Fall 2007); Terje I. Leiren, ed. and trans., *Selected Plays of Marcus Thrane* (Norwegian-American Historical Association, 2007); Terje I. Leiren, *Marcus Thrane: A Norwegian Radical in America* (Norwegian-American Historical Association, 1987).
94. *Newsletter* 134 (Fall 2009).
95. *Newsletter* 137 (Spring 2010).
96. *Newsletter* 139 (Fall 2010); *Newsletter* 142 (Summer 2011).
97. *Newsletter* 143 (Fall 2011).
98. "NAHA Welcomes New Editor," *Newsletter Currents* 169 (Summer 2018): 3; "Anna Peterson," Luther College, accessed 9 January 2025, https://www.luther.edu/faculty/anna-peterson; "Luther College Faculty Anna Peterson Named the Norwegian-American Historical Association's New Editor," Luther College, accessed 9 January 2025, https://www.luther.edu/news/anna-peterson-new-editor.
99. *2021 Annual Report*; Kristina Warner, "Moving Toward Digitization," *Newsletter Currents* 174 (Winter 2019): 2; Kristina Warner, "Out of the Archives, into the World," *Newsletter Currents* 180 (Summer 2021): 2; Kristina Warner, "Digitizing the Papers of O. E. Rølvaag," *NAS* 40 (2022): 180–88.
100. M. L. Hansen, *The Problem of the Third Generation Immigrant* (Augustana Historical Society, 1938), 9.
101. Marcus L. Hansen, "A Century of Norwegian-American Progress and the Future," *Norden* (Chicago), November 1932, clipping in possession of the author.
102. Lovoll, Promise Fulfilled, 72, 76.
103. Lovoll, 168.

TEACHING AND LEARNING

200 Years of Norwegian Immigration

MARKING A MILESTONE IN THE CLASSROOM

Rennesa Jessup

On the cover of the fall 2024 issue of *Vesterheim* magazine is an image of fifty-two people standing in the outline of the *Restauration* ship. This outline, laid out in paving stones in the courtyard of Vesterheim, the National Norwegian-American Museum and Folk Art School, represents the shape and size of the sloop that brought the first organized group of emigrating Norwegians to the United States in 1825.

Looking at the photo, one finds it hard to imagine so many people on an overseas voyage on a ship of that size. The image is a testament to the determination and strong convictions of that first group of Norwegians. I showed the picture to my students and asked them what motivated the emigrants to endure such a journey. This was the launching point as I began to teach about the 200th

Figure 1. Vesterheim's Restauration Plaza includes an outline in white paving stones in the size and shape of the original *Restauration* ship. To help commemorate the 200th anniversary of its sailing, exactly fifty-two Decorah Symra members and friends gathered for a photograph on the plaza. Photo courtesy of Vesterheim National Norwegian-American Museum, who thanks Symra for funding this photography project. The purpose of the Symra Literary Society is to continue the study and appreciation of the rich Scandinavian culture inherited by Americans of Nordic ancestry as it has done since 1907 and to promote literary study and research generally.

anniversary of Norwegians coming to America in the spring of 2025. This year, I aimed to help students reflect on their own personal connections to Norway, their Norwegian or other immigrant roots, the reasons people left Norway, and how our ancestors' decisions affect us today.

I integrated material about Norwegian immigration into each of the courses I taught in the spring semester of 2025 at Minnesota State University, Mankato: Introduction to the Nordic Countries, Elementary and Intermediate Norwegian II, and Scandinavian Film.

Introduction to the Nordic Countries is a 100-level introductory course, yet it is comprehensive, covering the geography, history, literature, art, and culture of Norway, Denmark, Sweden, Iceland, Finland, the Faroe Islands, and Greenland. Nordic emigration to America is a topic that we always cover in the history unit of the course. We read Vilhelm Moberg's historical novel *The Emigrants,* which describes the conditions driving a Swedish family and other members of their parish to emigrate to America in 1850. Students often have modern preconceptions of Sweden as a Nordic paradise, but when they begin reading *The Emigrants,* many are astounded by the dire conditions in Småland in the middle of the nineteenth century. This spring, one student wrote in a response paper that "farmers worked so hard for such low standards of living." The protagonist Karl Oskar's father, Nils Jakob's Son, is described as having fought to clear his farm field full of stones his whole life until a boulder crushes his leg, leaving him disabled and dependent on others.[1] Karl Oskar and his young wife Kristina then take over the farm, loaded with debt and a growing family, and struggle through drought years to produce enough to feed their family and his parents on a small parcel of land. When Karl Oskar tries to convince his wife that opportunities for them await in America, Kristina is hesitant. The death of one of their children finally sways her.

Students are often moved by these scenes of everyday life and everyday struggles. Many are surprised to read Moberg's description of the religious persecution of members of the Åkian sect trying to worship as they see fit. Others are amused by the scene of Karl Oskar's little brother Robert attempting to fake his death to escape his fate as a farmhand but are later appalled when he is brought to his employer, reprimanded and abused. They witness, through historical fiction, multiple motivations for seeking a new life abroad. Though *The Emigrants* is set in Sweden, we discuss the history of emigration from all of the Nordic countries and immigration to the United States more generally. This, in turn, inspires students to talk about their own family ancestry.

An extra reading assignment in my spring Norwegian courses was Paul Hasvold's transcribed speech "The Restauration Folk," printed in the same 2024 issue of *Vesterheim* magazine featuring the aforementioned cover photo. Paul

Hasvold was a Lutheran pastor in Decorah, Iowa, who was known for his presentation about the history of the *Restauration,* which he gave many times at Vesterheim. He provides an excellent overview of how and why this group of fifty-two Norwegians organized to emigrate overseas in 1825 and the many obstacles they encountered along the way and after they arrived.

As this was originally a speech, the oral storytelling-style of the article resonated with the students, and they reported finding it informative and entertaining to read. They were shocked to find that every passenger survived the journey, despite the fact that the voyage took ninety-eight days. Another surprise was the southerly route of the ship and the fact that the emigrants "were packed in like sardines."[2] One student wrote, "Every new chapter of their journey was more difficult and challenging than the last," and yet the passengers endured and did not let their spirits fade, even when they were fined upon their arrival in New York. Many students were surprised to learn about the religious motivations of those aboard the *Restauration,* given modern Norway's reputation as a secular society. Others were surprised that Quakers were considered radical and that the people following the Haugean movement were not allowed to hold religious meetings even though they were Lutherans. I always point out to my students that Hauge Lutheran Church, in Kenyon, Minnesota, still stands as a legacy of the Haugean movement that Norwegians brought to America.

This reading assignment and a class discussion were followed by a reflective questionnaire designed to help students think about what they know, and what they do not know, about their ancestry. Do they know from where, when, or why their ancestors came to the United States? Have they heard any family stories? Are there any cultural traditions in their families related to their ethnic heritage (such as foods for special occasions, activities, or handcrafts)? Do they have family heirlooms related to their heritage? Do they know if any family members spoke another language when they arrived and how long the language was spoken in their family? Do any family members currently speak a heritage language?

These questions prompted quite a variety of responses. Some students knew few or no details of their family history, and some had quite detailed stories. Several reported Norwegian or Scandinavian ancestry but also German,

Greek, Polish, Czech, Irish, Scottish, Dutch, and others. These were all students in a Norwegian language course, but none of those with Norwegian ancestry had learned any Norwegian from family members. One student reported having a grandfather, born in the United States to German parents, who spoke German at home until he went to school. Another reported that her grandfather was born in Minnesota to Norwegian-speaking parents but did not learn to speak Norwegian himself. However, when she tried speaking some Norwegian phrases to her grandfather, he broke out into a bright smile of recognition. Several students mentioned making or eating *lefse* and *krumkake* as family traditions, but few other remnants of cultural practice were mentioned.

In my Scandinavian Film course, students watched *Brudeferden i Hardanger* (The bridal party in Hardanger), a 1926 silent film directed by Rasmus Breistein and based on Kristofer Janson's 1868 novel *Marit Skjølte.*[3] The beginning intertitle reads, "Det var på den tiden da Amerikafeberen herjet som verst i Norge" (It all happened in the days when the America fever raged in Norway).

Figure 2. A still shot from the 1926 silent film *Brudeferden i Hardanger* (The bridal party in Hardanger). Courtesy of the Norwegian National Library.

This opens to a shot of a couple rowing out to meet a ship, the woman waving a handkerchief to presumed loved ones ashore.

It is departure day for America. Marit, a young woman, set to emigrate with her parents, runs away from the dock at the last moment because she cannot bear to leave her sweetheart. Her parents, seeing the ship preparing to depart, are forced to leave without her. From a mountaintop, she watches the ship disappear into the distance. She will never see her family again. The film invites us to question her choice. The "bridal party" of the title turns out to be not Marit's but that of another woman who marries Marit's sweetheart. The powerful scene in which she watches her parents depart emphasizes the reality of emigration: some family members stay and others leave. We are here today, and others are in Norway, because of those choices.

Rennesa Jessup *is professor of Scandinavian studies at Minnesota State University, Mankato.*

NOTES

1. Vilhelm Moberg, *The Emigrants,* trans. Gustav Lannestock (Borealis, 1995), 5.
2. Paul Hasvold, "The Restauration Folk," *Vesterheim* 22, no. 2 (2024): 7.
3. *Brudeferden i Hardanger,* dir. Rasmus Breistein (1926; Kommunenes Filmcentral A/S. Norsk filminstitutt, 2007), available at Nasjonalbiblioteket, https://urn.nb.no/URN:NBN:no-nb_video_6531; Kristofer Janson, *Marit Skjølte* (Bergen, Norway: Giertsen, 1868).

Bodil Stenseth. *Muus vs. Muus: The Scandal That Shook Norwegian America.* Edited by Kari Lie Dorer. Translated by Kari Lie Dorer and Torild Homstad.
Minnesota Historical Society Press and Norwegian American Historical Association, 2024. 368 pages.

Gracia Grindal

This is Kari Lie Dorer and Torild Homstad's translation of the Norwegian book *Fru Muus' Klage: Ekteskapsskandalen som rystet det norske Amerika* by Bodil Stenseth (reviewed by me in *Norwegian-American Studies* 39 [2021]), with further editing and text by Dorer. The subject is Oline Muus versus her husband Bernt Julius Muus. Mr. Muus, founder of St. Olaf College and longtime pastor of Holden congregation near Northfield, Minnesota, was a leader in the Norwegian Lutheran Church. When his wife engaged a lawyer, the young Andrew Ueland, to help her with the legal issues surrounding her inheritance from her father in Norway, a huge scandal ensued. In Norway, the inheritance would have gone to her husband, who owned it as the head of the family. In America, however, the wife could inherit it in her own right. This was the issue that started the women's rights movement when women—like Cady Stanton, daughter of a wealthy man—fought to inherit their fathers' estates even after they married and became, as they said, "civilly dead." They had gotten laws passed so that women could inherit their families' wealth, putting an end to lotharios courting rich young women for their fortunes and running off with it, giving the young, abandoned wife no legal recourse.

Mrs. Muus's complaint against her husband intrigued her lawyer, who saw it as a way to make his reputation. Then it spun out of control in the press, in the courts, and in public opinion, leaving the two main characters struggling to maintain their reputations and their own sanity. The legal complaint was clear-cut: Was Norwegian law applicable for Norwegian citizens in America, or did American law rule?

Ueland, however, decided that the court of public opinion would help his case, so he had Mrs. Muus write a letter (or did he?) about her husband's treatment of her. It was well written and shocking but had very little to do with the actual case. Immediately, the press, both Norwegian and English, got involved, and the sensational charges between the two created intense public interest. The press—secular and churchly—went at it hammer and tongs. There was war between the several church bodies, especially the Norwegian Synod at Luther College and the Conference at Augsburg Seminary, who were happy to enter the lists. Then there were those, like Ueland and Luther Jaeger, editor of *Budstikken,* who were not very friendly to the church and regarded this as a fight between the hidebound Norwegian Synod and the freedom being fought for by the suffragettes, whom they instinctively supported.

As the proceedings continued with increasingly tense and sensational meetings in the Holden church and more revelations in the press, one came to know more about the couple than is wholesome. As heir to that world of gossip, I have heard awful things not mentioned here, but while credible, none of it was substantiated. After a lifetime of reading about this, I cannot decide what was true about them, especially since Mrs. Muus withdrew her most flagrant accusation at the end. The book, which is a model of good historical writing, does not help, nor could it.

Dorer has added more research to her version of Stenseth that gives the debate a bit more nuance: more on Mr. Muus at St. Olaf, how Georg Sverdrup and Sven Oftedal at Augsburg took Mrs. Muus's part and were kind to her, plus an afterword that gives us insight into the author's coming to know this story. I am bothered by the presentation of the case as being between the sacred and the secular; this is also a churchly debate in which two contending and fractious sides of Norwegian Lutheranism seized on this unhappy story to prosecute their cases against each other. Neither writer looked at *Folkebladet,* edited by Sven Oftedal at Augsburg. *Folkebladet* took the Norwegian Lutheran liberal pro-suffrage side of the argument that would make the arguments seem not just church versus world but also intra-Norwegian Lutheran churches. That is, to my mind, the major flaw of the book, both the original and the translation.

There are minor mistakes that show that neither author nor translators fully understand the religious context, such as that *Luther's Small Catechism* bound with Erick Pontoppidan's *Explanation* with its over 700 questions was fundamental to Norwegian Lutheran confirmation rites, a terrifying puberty rite. To my mind, the authors too easily receive the old prejudice: Norwegian Synod = bad, freethinkers (like Jaeger) = good. To paint the brawling Norwegian Lutherans in America as all the same misses the massive library of publications within the community for over a century that give us a richer, more textured tradition that too many miss.

Still, it is a page-turner and very well done.

Gracia Grindal *is professor emerita of rhetoric from Luther Seminary in St. Paul, Minnesota. She is a poet, hymn text writer, and writer of Norwegian-American women's biographies.*

Shannon Egan and Marthe Tolnes Fjellestad, editors. *Across the West and Toward the North: Norwegian and American Landscape Photography.*
University of Utah Press, 2022. 260 pages.

Justin Carville

W. J. T. Mitchell's call to shift the study of landscape as a genre of pictorial representation to a medium of cultural transformation by changing the understanding of the term *landscape* from a noun to a verb—*to landscape*—encapsulates the essays exploring the transnational relations between Norwegian and American landscape photography from the second half of the nineteenth century in the lavishly illustrated *Across the West and Toward the North.*[1] Published to accompany the traveling exhibition of the same title, the collective aim of the essays is to reflect on the historical, aesthetic, and political affinities between landscape photography of the frontiers of the American West and Northern Norway. Through four thematic essays exploring issues across gender, technology, tourism, and transcultural modernism, and five short comparative essays pairing landscape photographs from Norway and America, the publication identifies the emergence of similar visual motifs and cross-cultural practices of landscape photography in both nations.

Shannon Egan's comprehensive introduction outlines the scope of these affinities, identifying shared visual motifs, aesthetic correspondences, and compositional parallels between American and Norwegian landscape photographs while acknowledging their historical and contextual divergences in the photographic iterations of national identity. Each of the four longer essays explores aspects of these shared motifs as they intersect with other cultural formations of landscape imaginaries. James R. Swensen's "Ragged Places and Rugged Men" explores how the physical and technological challenges of accessing and photographing the American West offered opportunities to affirm and express white settler masculinity through spaces of frontier exploration. Focusing on how modern transportation networks of roads and railways opened the Norwegian landscape to cultural tourism and the entwining of conceptualizations of nature and culture, Torild Gjesvik's "Traveling with Knud Knudsen"—a photographer whose work features prominently in the book—examines how photographic excursions not only provided a position from which the photographer expressed their experience of the Norwegian landscape for the viewer but also became visual motifs that codified the intersection of modernization and nature. In "Getting Soaked at Yellowstone," Elizabeth Hutchinson considers the interaction of cultural tourists with the material environment of Yellowstone National Park in the work of a number of photographers, including the Norwegian Anders Beer Wilse, not only as a visual motif in their photographs but also as the endeavor of transporting the physical apparatus and chemical solutions through the challenging terrain of the American West to produce the visual imagining of Yellowstone. Trond Erik Bjorli's exploration of the Norwegian-American photographer Anders Beer Wilse's interest in the *vidden* motif in his photographs of the high mountain areas of Norway makes the case for a transnational aesthetic modernism in Wilse's photographic work that entwines the physical and emotive responses to nature. Each of these contributors and Egan make up the authors of the five short comparative essays that cover topics such as dwellings, photographers, glaciers, railways, and human settlement across American and Norwegian landscape photography.

Each of the contributors brings their own particular disciplinary perspective to the range of shared transcultural affinities outlined in the introduction, offering differing routes into the terrains of landscape imagery across the Atlantic. Gjesvik's essay on Knudsen, for example, outlines the photographer's visit to the 1893 Chicago World's Columbian Exposition as a departure point to explore the connections between travel, photographic practice, and shifting sensibilities of the modern landscape. Linking travel, infrastructural engineering, amateur trekking associations, and commercial cultural tourism, Gjesvik identifies the road as not only providing access to the landscape but also an orientation of the gaze that is reflected in Knudsen's myopic focus on the materiality of the marks of mobility and transportation routes that mark the landscape. There are also insights into how shifts in road design from the French principle of relatively straight roads with steep gradients to the emergence of the chaussée in the mid-nineteenth century, which followed more undulating routes through the terrain, contributed to the formal qualities of Norwegian landscape photography.

With the exception of Hutchinson's short essay discussing John K. Hillers's photograph of the Native American Zuni village in Pueblo, New Mexico, and Knud Knudsen's image of a Sámi supply storage dwelling, both from the 1870s, and Egan's discussion of ethnographic tourism, Indigenous space receives little in-depth discussion. Egan's introduction notes that the doctrine of Manifest Destiny and the narrative of settler colonialism that accompanies imagery of the American West does not have a corresponding history of colonial violence in Norway, while acknowledging the emergence of Norwegian nationalism after it ceded from Denmark. In this sense, it works around the type of transcultural history of photography and settler colonialism between America and the Tasman world recently explored by Jarrod Hore, which makes a compelling link between the cultural uses and aesthetics of photography, the geographical imaginary of settler colonialism, and the dispossession of Indigenous culture.[2] With the exception of Swensen's acknowledgment of women's role in the surveys of the American West, the spaces of landscape photography in both nations are also portrayed as deeply masculine. In the Norwegian context, Sigrid Lien and Hilde Wallem Nielssen's research on women photographers in the Sámi communities and border territories of the north offers an interesting alternative to this absence of women in addition to foregrounding photography's complicity with the violence of the cultural politics of the Norwegianization of the Sámi.[3] *Across the West* thus has its own lacuna, but as an accompanying publication to an exhibition it has a specific job to do expanding upon and moving beyond the themes of the exhibit. The essays, both long and short, make a valuable companion to these other histories of photography by deepening transnational scholarship of landscape photography as it is incorporated into the cultural politics of nation-building across America and Norway.

Justin Carville *teaches historical and theoretical studies in photography at the Institute of Art, Design and Technology in Dún Laoghaire, Ireland.*

NOTES

1. W. J. T. Mitchell, introduction to *Landscape and Power,* ed. W. J. T. Mitchell (University of Chicago Press, 1994), 1.
2. Jarrod Hore, *Visions of Nature: How Landscape Photography Shaped Settler Colonialism* (University of California Press, 2022).
3. Sigrid Lien and Hilde Wallem Nielssen, "Camera Encounters: Bourgeois Settler Women's Adventures in Sámi Areas of Norway," in *Adjusting the Lens: Indigenous Activism, Colonial Legacies, and Photographic Heritage,* ed. Sigrid Lien and Hilde Wallem Nielssen (University of British Columbia Press, 2021).

Odd S. Lovoll. *Colonel Hans Christian Heg and the Norwegian American Experience.*
Minnesota Historical Society Press, 2023. 224 pages.

Kristin A. Risley

As the bicentennial of organized Norwegian migration to North America is celebrated in 2025, it is a good time to read the first full-length biography of one of Norwegian America's enduring heroes, Civil War Colonel Hans Christian Heg of the Fifteenth Wisconsin Infantry Regiment (the "Scandinavian Regiment"), who gave his life in service to the Union at the Battle of Chickamauga in September 1863. The book is authored by one of the leading scholars of Norwegian-American history, Odd S. Lovoll.

In the preface, Lovoll discusses the exigence of his project: the vandalism, decapitation, and removal of the Heg statue in Madison on 23 June 2020 following George Floyd protests near the Wisconsin State Capitol. The statue was eventually dumped in nearby Lake Monona. Lovoll explains that "the attack on the Heg statue demanded biographical documentation" of Heg's life, and the book serves to educate a new generation of readers about Heg's experience: His early life in Norway, his youth in Wisconsin during "the formative years of Norwegian immigration" and settlement, and his dynamic leadership that led to a varied career and military fame (2).

Following his wartime contributions and sacrifice, Heg became a nucleus for public memory for more than a century. Fittingly, Lovoll frames his text with key commemorations. The book opens with two centennials that took place in Minnesota and featured the Fifteenth Wisconsin Regiment as a "symbol and source of great ethnic pride": the 1914 centennial to honor the signing of the Norwegian Constitution and the Norse-American Centennial of 1925 that mythologized the life of Colonel Heg in a dramatic pageant, praising him as a model citizen (5, 7). The book ends with the 1920s dedications of three sister statues of Colonel Heg, one in Norway and two in Wisconsin, and the 2022 rededication of the Heg statue in Madison.

The biography has five chronological chapters, each of which explores a discrete phase of Heg's experience. The production is of fine quality: Attractive cover art features a photograph of the colonel in uniform, and the text is augmented by a rich variety of figures and archival materials. Heg family artifacts elevate the book's interest. Lovoll's prose style and translations of Norwegian-language texts provide clarity and accessibility for all readers.

The first chapter explores the Heg family origins in Norway and the social, economic, and religious forces, such as the Haugean reform movement, that shaped Heg's early life and led the family to emigrate. Lovoll notes that "historical narratives frequently neglect . . . the immigrants' homeland," an omission that he remedies with ample context (2). The second chapter showcases the author's vast knowledge of Norwegian immigration history as he chronicles the Muskego settlement in southern Wisconsin. Founded by Norwegians in 1839, Muskego served as "a mother colony" and gateway to other settlements in the Midwest (44). The Hegs arrived in 1840, and father Even Hansen Heg "did much to build up the colony" and establish ethnic institutions that undoubtedly shaped his son's "political convictions" (41, 67). Newly arrived immigrants lodged in the Heg barn, which also served as a church and a hospital; the first Norwegian-language newspaper in America, *Nordlyset* (The northern light), was printed in the Heg home in 1847 (51, 65). Lovoll underscores the vital role of the immigrant press as a "political tool for newcomers," a theme that continues in the third chapter, which traces Heg's political career and antislavery affiliations with the Free Soil Party and early Republican Party (68). The portrayal of Heg as a media-savvy politico—giving speeches, writing letters to newspapers, and enacting reforms as a capable prison commissioner—is compelling.

In the last two chapters, Lovoll contributes to scholarship on ethnic regiments in the Civil War, arguing that the military service of ethnic groups represented "the ultimate initiation into American culture and history" (113). At the same time, Heg's recruiting activities and the Norwegian ethos of the Fifteenth Wisconsin manifest "a public and national marking of a Norwegian ethnic identity" that had been evolving in the years leading up to the war (116). Lovoll builds on the work of Theodore C. Blegen and other Norwegian-American historians and merges early histories of the Fifteenth Wisconsin with recent studies. At times, however, the book relies too heavily on older sources, such as E. B. Quiner's *The Military History of Wisconsin* (1866), and falls short of providing a cohesive discussion of Heg's military campaigns. Civil War enthusiasts will find little new information here. Another missed opportunity is the integration of authoritative primary sources in English, such as the *Official Records*. Nevertheless, Lovoll is not writing "traditional military history," nor does the book provide a conventional biography so much as a cultural history in which readers may expect to learn much about the Norwegian-American experience as reflected in Heg's life and "lasting legacy" (3).

Kristin A. Risley *is professor of English at the University of Wisconsin–Stout. Her scholarly interests include American literature, ethnic studies, and public memory research on the Colonel Heg monuments. She served as a Fulbright Professor of American Literature and Culture at the University of Bergen in 2006–2007.*

NOTES FROM THE FIELD

Reflections on the (Bi-)Centennial Celebrations

Terje Leiren

The year 2025 commemorates a double anniversary for Norwegian Americans. It marks the bicentennial of the first organized emigration from Norway to North America and the centennial of the founding of the Norwegian American Historical Association. Both events have proven to be significant historical events not only in the United States and Canada, where the majority of the emigrants settled, but also in Norway. Many of those who celebrated the centennial of the 1825 arrival of the small sloop *Restauration* were themselves immigrants, giving them a close personal connection to the migration experience. Desiring that the struggles and successes of the Norwegian immigrants in the new country be remembered, the idea formed to establish "an historical agency which might collect and preserve records and objects that throw light upon the activities and backgrounds of this element in the American population."[1] Consequently, in the wake of the 1925 "slooper centennial celebrations," the Norwegian American Historical Association was born. When the first volume of *Studies and Records* was published in 1926, it listed 566 members.

To acknowledge the connections between Norway and the new homeland of the emigrants and their descendants, Norway also commemorates special occasions, such as the bicentennial, by sending artists, authors, musicians, scholars, and, in some cases, government officials to represent and inform about modern Norway. North Americans of Norwegian descent, however, may or may not maintain a continuing connection with their ancestral homeland or shared heritage, but to those that do, the dual commemorations in 2025 are significant markers deemed worthy of remembering and even celebrating.

CROSSINGS
NORWAY & NORTH AMERICA
1825 • 2025

Figure 1. A transatlantic committee developed the Crossings logo with Replace design firm of Minneapolis. The logo is available to partner organizations in English, Norwegian, Sámi, and French.

In an essay on collective memory and ethnic groups, the historian John Bodnar writes that collective memory "is a body of beliefs and ideas about the past that allows an entire social group to interpret and understand its present."[2] By doing so, individuals in that group may connect more fully with their heritage and thereby also gain insight into their own cultural identity. As a result, family ties may be strengthened and generational gaps bridged. Preserving and celebrating our heritage will allow future generations to build their own identities using what we leave them as a foundation.

Ironically, the 1925 celebrations occurred in the wake of the passing of several restrictive immigration acts in 1924 that included the Johnson–Reed Act, the Asian Exclusion Act, and the National Origins Act. A quota system was put into place along with a consular control system for visas in order for future immigrants to enter the country. The United States Border Patrol was also established. The celebrations in 2025 seem to echo in the cultural context of a renewed push by the national government to limit or discourage immigration. So, is there value in celebrating the two centennials and, if so, to what extent?

Anniversaries are celebrations of historical events that may evoke our emotions and fire our imagination. As individuals or as a group, anniversaries can infuse our memory and reinforce our identity if we let them. They allow us to make connections with the past while also looking forward, thereby gaining the opportunity to reexamine and reflect on the events themselves, sometimes in new ways with new methodologies, new insights, and new theories.

The centennial celebration of the founding of the Norwegian American Historical Association can serve as an avenue to greater public participation, dialogue, and debate in the understanding of the history of Norwegian emigration to and settlement and development of Norwegians in North America. The celebration of the bicentennial of Norwegian emigration includes not only the migration story but also an opportunity to reflect on the changes in Norway itself. In 1825, Norway was a relatively poor country, seemingly compelling its people to emigrate. In 2025, however, Norway has come to be one of the wealthiest, most modern, sophisticated, egalitarian, and scientifically advanced countries in the world. That journey is also worthy of celebration in the bicentennial year.

Terje Leiren *is professor emeritus of Scandinavian studies and history at the University of Washington, Seattle. In addition to several books and numerous scholarly articles, he is the author of two books published by the Norwegian American Historical Association on the nineteenth-century Norwegian-American radical Marcus Thrane.*

NOTES

1. D. G. Ristad, "The Norwegian-American Historical Association," in *The Norwegian-American Historical Association Studies and Records,* vol. 1 (1926), 148.
2. John Bodnar, "Collective Memory and Ethnic Groups: The Case of Swedes, Mennonites, and Norwegians," in *Swensen Swedish Immigration Research Center Occasional Papers* (Swenson Swedish Immigration Research Center, 1991), 7.

Literature from Minnesota

University of Minnesota Press | www.upress.umn.edu | 800-621-2736

The Rocks Will Echo Our Sorrow

The Forced Displacement of the Northern Sámi

Elin Anna Labba

Translated by Fiona Graham

"Sámi journalist Labba makes the trauma of the forced removal of her people from northern Norway and Sweden both palpable and painful in this profound debut history." —***Publisher's Weekly***, starred review

$22.95 hardcover | 208 pages

Accidental Shepherd

How a California Girl Rescued an Ancient Mountain Farm in Norway

Liese Greensfelder

"Emphasizes the value of tradition and community." —***Library Journal***, starred

$27.95 hardcover | 280 pages

The Complete and Original Norwegian Folktales of Asbjørnsen and Moe

Peter Christen Asbjørnsen and Jørgen Moe

Translated by Tiina Nunnally

The definitive English translation of the celebrated story collection regarded as a **landmark of Norwegian literature and culture**—now in paperback

$29.95 paperback | 344 pages

The Palace of the Snow Queen

Winter Travels in Lapland and Sápmi

Barbara Sjoholm

"A captivating homage to the frozen far North and the Sámi." —***Booklist***

$18.95 paperback | 352 pages

Olav Audunssøn

IV. Winter

Sigrid Undset

Translated by Tiina Nunnally

"Should be read by anyone who wants to learn about an important period in Norwegian history and, at the same time, to read a very thrilling story." —***Norwegian American***

$17.95 paperback | 352 pages

ALSO AVAILABLE:

I. Vows, II. Providence, III. Crossroads